PROMOTE YOUR INNER COWGIRL

PROMOTE
your inner
COWGIRL

**THE HORSE LOVER'S WAY TO WORK LESS,
EARN MORE, & LIVE YOUR PASSION**

DR. LYNDA FLOWERS

NEW YORK

LONDON • NASHVILLE • MELBOURNE • VANCOUVER

Promote Your Inner Cowgirl

The Horse Lover's Way to Work Less, Earn More, and Live Your Passion

Published in New York, New York, by Morgan James Publishing in partnership with Difference Press. Morgan James is a trademark of Morgan James, LLC. www.MorganJamesPublishing.com

ISBN 9781642798951 paperback
ISBN 9781642798968 eBook
Library of Congress Control Number: 2019953451

Cover Design Concept:
Jennifer Stinson

Cover Design by:
Megan Dillon
megan@creativeninjadesigns.com

Interior Design by:
Christopher Kirk
www.GFSstudio.com

Editor:
Todd Hunter

Book Coaching:
The Author Incubator

Morgan James is a proud partner of Habitat for Humanity Peninsula and Greater Williamsburg. Partners in building since 2006.

Get involved today! Visit
MorganJamesPublishing.com/giving-back

For Tommy, Emma, and Cori,
my loving and boldly honest children.
Thank you for helping to mold me into a strong leader
by being courageous enough to call me out on my stuff.
I love you all, evenly and uniquely.

TABLE OF CONTENTS

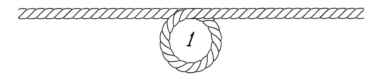

HOBBLED TO THE HITCHING POST

Some people grin and bear it.
Other people smile and change it.

There you are, sitting at the same desk in the same cubicle working on the same computer, trying to figure out how you can afford to buy the new saddle, go to the horse show this weekend, and pay your bills. Your house also needs some cleaning and a few minor repairs, which will cost a pretty penny, but you'd rather spend that money on your horses. Not only that, hay is going to be expensive this year, so you need to figure out where to find the extra money, so you don't end up with garbage round bales. And then there are spring shots along with the deworming and Coggins tests. Why, oh why does your passion cost so much more than you earn? Is it even worth it?

And then there's your marriage. Even though your husband knew about your horse addiction long before you got married, you can feel him becoming more and more irritated with your horse spending. He wants to take an extended weekend getaway to the Bahamas, and that's the last place you want to go. Baking on the beach in the sun sounds boring compared to hanging out with your horses and horse friends at a rodeo or on a trail ride. You'd rather save your money so you can enjoy a shopping spree at the Quarter Horse Congress and get tickets for the coveted two-year-old Master's class. You love your husband, but he just doesn't seem to understand your passion for horses. And, you're tired of trying to hide your horse spending from him.

If only you had some extra money so you could get the new silver show saddle and go to a few shows. Even a few local open shows would be fun. Instead, you have to work this job of yours, sitting in this grey-walled office, answering phone calls, talking to people who complain about pretty much everything, just so you can pay the hay bill. It's getting frustrating. It's sapping your energy, and it's tugging on your last nerve. You're tired of feeling hobbled to the school horse hitching post.

As you drive home, you wonder aloud if you should ask for a raise, or if you should consider getting a better job. Your husband will blow his stack if you even think for a second about switching jobs again. Somehow you have to figure out how to make more money and get Fridays off so you can go to the shows, or go trail riding, or just clean the barn. Then, you realize that this is the same conversation you've had with yourself so many times before in the past six months. You sigh and let out a deep, growly breath. You realize that something has to change. You are tired of working all week, racing home on Friday night to get ready for the show on Saturday, and having to hear your husband complain about how much time and money you're spending on your horses. Something has to give.

You have a nice resume, bursting with accomplishments. You've won company awards and have accolades from your boss and clients for your efforts. You've been fully trained and know you could run the whole office by yourself. But, you don't really want the added responsibility and time that you'll have to spend there.

You have the skills to multi-task because that's what your whole life is – multi-tasking. You juggle your career, your marriage, your kids, your health, and your horses. Sure, life could be less hectic, but you are a high-achiever and a competitor at heart. And, you're tired. Tired of running on the rat-race treadmill all week just so you can enjoy a few minutes with your horses on weekends.

You know something needs to change. Do you ask for a raise or figure out something else? You're tired of starting over. You wonder how your friends can afford their horses. It's probably because they don't have to do it on their own. They have support from their wealthy parents, or their husband. You have neither. Maybe you should throw in the towel and be happy with your Breyer horse collection. At least they don't eat expensive hay and leave piles of poop all over. But you know deep down that your heart and soul would wither without your pasture buddies.

You consider whether you should start a side business. That would give you more money and eventually more freedom. But, you aren't sure what you could do and it seems risky. You've tried a couple of MLM (multilevel marketing) companies, but those didn't work out too well. You sold a few products to your friends and family but couldn't seem to get people to sign up under you and ended up spending just as much money as you made, or maybe more. Not only that, your husband might not be supportive of you starting your own business since you couldn't even make an MLM work.

Still, you figure that if you started a side business and it grew, you could quit your job in six months or a year, and your life would be so much better. You could call your own shots and decide your own schedule. You could go to the barn every day and go to a show or trail ride when you wanted. You know you'd be so much happier spending that time with your horses. And, you wouldn't be so crabby with your husband and family.

Starting your own business would mean so many positive things for you. You would finally be excited about working because you'd be working for yourself, not someone else. You could make an impact, do what you want, and not get stuck doing the mundane tasks that nobody else wants to do. Mostly, you'd have control over your schedule, and that means having the freedom to go to the barn, to shows, to a rodeo, or trail riding.

You know you have leadership and management skills because you manage your household and horses, and you do it well. You know that you could manage a business also. You just need a framework and an idea. You know you'll have a renewed sense of satisfaction with your business and even feel like you're making a difference.

Perhaps the greatest aspect of starting a business will be the impact you will be able to make on other people. You could teach them new skills, or provide a service that horse lovers need, or sell a product that you already use and love. You believe you could do it, but you also know that your husband probably won't support you and your friends are tired of your MLM offerings.

At some point you have to figure out if it's all worth it – the long job hours, the stress, and the toll your job is taking on your health, marriage, and horses. Mentally, you're about at your end. You can't keep having these conversations out loud with yourself as you commute to and from work. You get yourself mad and riled up, feeling your stress levels rise and your heart pound, but you just aren't totally certain what you need to do. After all, what if you start a business and it flops? Then what? You could always ask for a raise at work. That's safe. But if you get it, then you will also have more responsibility and get sucked deeper into your job so much that you don't even have time for your horses. Then do you stay and accept where you are? You just don't think that's an option. You would become even more bitter and worn out. No, you know you need to do something else. Find another job or start your own business.

You're pretty sure your husband won't be happy if you quit your job, even though you're going to find another one. The lag in income will certainly take a toll on your marriage, family life, and horses. But, this job is already taking a toll on you. Some days you find it difficult to get motivated to get out of bed and go to work. Even though you like what you do, you just can't seem to shake the desire to be in the barn. One thing is for certain; you'll never shake that desire.

It's time to make a decision. I understand where you are and what you're feeling. I've been there too. I can assure you that if you follow the steps that you're about to learn, you will regain your excitement, refocus your efforts, and finally get to live your passion. The inner arguments, the physical and mental health strain, and the over-worked weekends will fade away. You will have a fresh, new perspective on where you're going, how you're getting there, and who you are. Let's get going. It's time to get unhobbled from the school horse hitching post so you can start your journey.

2

LEADERSHIP: THE COWGIRL WAY

Makin' it in life is kinda like bustin' broncs: you're gonna get thrown a lot. The simple secret is to keep gettin' back on because you don't learn much when everything goes right.

'm pretty sure I came out of the womb as a horse lover. When I was young, I had a huge Breyer horse collection with a few token Barbies to care for the horses and maybe ride them. I made reins for my bicycle handlebars so I could pretend my bike was a horse. I even posted, pretending to be trotting, as I pedaled my two-wheeler around the block. I spent hours reading every horse training book I could find at the library. Whenever

I went to visit my grandpa who was a farmer, I rode his Hackney pony, Dusty. And, if he was too busy to help me, I dragged the western saddle out to a big log in the front pasture, carefully positioned it on the log and rode in that saddle all day, imagining I was riding and training my own horses. Funny how I never got tired of sitting in that saddle. Horses were in my blood.

After my grandpa had a freak accident with Dusty, the pony went down the road, and I had to go back to my Breyer horse collection. I spent years begging for a horse from my parents. A pony was always at the top of my Christmas list, but somehow Santa never brought me a real live one. Finally, when I was 12 years old, after having to attend my fifth different school (a dangerous middle school) due to family moves, my parents agreed to let me buy my own horse. I spent my $700 life-savings on a huge Saddlebred. I was in heaven, or so I thought. He tried to kill me nearly every time I rode him by bolting and then scraping me off by running against a fence or ducking under a low tree branch or anything else he could find. He scared me to death!

Fast forward a year and another family move, Lucky O'Dare had become my best friend. I had no stable group of friends and had to make a new best friend every year. I found out that my horse was truly my best friend. He was the shoulder I cried on and my confidant. We spent hours riding all over the countryside. We ran barrels, jumped obstacles, performed dressage patterns, raced through fields, and ordered french fries through the McDonald's drive through.

After attending a different school nearly every year and changing friends so many times, I lost who I was. By the time I was in college, I was even more confused about who I was. My parents were expecting me to go to medical school but my heart was really with my horse. I had decided that I wanted to work with horses but was told that there was no money in that and it could never support any kind of decent lifestyle. I was working for a horse trainer, riding and showing, and loving every minute of it. We also bred mares and worked with the foals. I loved the horses and horse shows so much that it really didn't matter that I didn't have gobs of money because I loved my life.

I ended up not following my passions, but instead being the good daughter and following the lucrative career path, which ended up not working for me anyway. I continually made choices that were not in alignment with myself. I honored other people's suggestions, which blinded me to myself, and my choices kept getting worse and worse, ending in two failed marriages and a career that paid the bills but didn't light up my soul.

By the time I was in my 30s, I had also started a business that was wildly successful, grossing over $1 million in sales the first year. This worked perfectly while

I started raising a family. However, sometimes life has other plans, and I soon found myself in a nasty divorce, that left me with no business, no home, no car, and no income. I had my two-year-old daughter and that was what mattered. We moved into my parents' basement, and I went on public aide until I could regroup and restart.

I learned some hard lessons during this time. I learned that I could survive with very few possessions. I learned who really cared about me, which ended up being a small number. Nonetheless, I learned that these were my people and my supporters. As some people come and go in our lives, these people are still with me today, except for my grandparents who have since passed away. Finding and keeping your people is one of the most important personal care actions you can take. These people may or may not be blood relatives, and that doesn't matter. What matters is that they will be there to help you no matter what.

I did a lot of soul searching as I tried to figure out what was wrong with me and what other people had that I didn't have. Some people told me I should go back to school, take a sales job or work in corporate but when I did any of these things, deep down I wasn't happy even though I was good at school and sales. I tried to hold up a mirror to myself and see the reflection through their eyes because I figured they must know something I didn't.

A glance into the mirror took me onto a five-year journey of self-help books. I simply had to figure out what was wrong with me and why I had so many failures. Every self-help book I read, from boundary setting to finding happiness to finding my true calling talked about making better choices, tuning into your gut, and seeking truth through getting in touch with the universe. I meditated. I prayed. I tried yoga. I loved all those things, but they did not seem to get me any closer to figuring out what was wrong with me.

I even enrolled in a coach training program to accompany a friend through the program. I was a high-achiever, getting things done, earning college degrees and certifications with no effort, so I figured I had just read one too many self-help books and maybe I was chasing my tail. However, through the coach training, I learned a few things. I learned that there really wasn't anything wrong with me other than lacking some communication skills that I hadn't learned in my childhood. I learned I could trust my gut and that my insight was amazingly keen. My frustrations at failing so many times morphed into a curiosity and, eventually, gratitude for the journey that I had chosen in order to solve some life riddles. Most importantly, I learned that being the black sheep of the family meant that many times I was the only one seeing the white elephant (relational dysfunctions) in the room, and that scared people.

When I trusted my gut and intuition, I learned that I had a special knack for seeing through behaviors into underlying motivating factors and dysfunctions. Certain people around me were comfortable with the big white elephant. I, on the other hand, was tired of stepping in elephant poop.

I was tired of being told by various family members that I had problems and being labeled as ungrateful or disrespectful. Of course I had problems! We all did, but I was the only one who wanted the problems resolved. For some, the white elephant is a story they tell themselves about how important they are, or how hard they work, or how smart they are. If you disrupt the story, then you're suddenly mean and uncaring. Many times, these people are insecure and have taken on a narcissistic disorder so that they can feel okay looking in their mirror. For me, the white elephant is a big message that something or someone is not authentic, loving, and caring. Some people avoid looking at the white elephant because they don't want to do the work of resolving problems and fixing relationships. If you point out this big elephant, then you're either crazy or mean or both. You also risk broken relationships and being called all kinds of names with disrespectful and ungrateful being near the top of the list. Pointing out that white elephant is scary to some people because they've befriended their elephant and can't risk losing their identity.

Over the past 30 years, I've started or acquired quite a few businesses. I've worked in sales, management, retail, small business, professional coaching, and health care. I was part owner in an art gallery, a chain of vitamin stores, beauty salons, a mortgage flipping business, a vending business, a packaging and printing business, and a coaching business. My first business in 1985 was selling a business start-up manual, which grossed a whopping $400 in three months over my college summer break. The business that grossed over $1 million in sales the first year was a packaging and printing business. The mortgage flipping and gumball businesses never made it out of the red. Some of my ventures were successful, and some were utter failures, but they all lacked my horse passion. I was missing the most important key to success: passion.

You can probably do a lot of different things and do them well. I ran beauty salons, was a massage therapist, and did makeup, nails, facials, and body waxing. I even won an award for the design of one of my stores. The layout became the national prototype for the product distributorship. I was good at all of that, but it didn't light me up. You might find yourself working in a job that you can do well but doesn't light up your soul. Just because you can do it well, doesn't mean it's the thing you should be doing. Let that sink in for a moment. *Just because you can do something better than a lot of people does not mean you should do it if it doesn't fill your heart.* It's purely a distraction.

I know where you are, feeling stuck in a job that doesn't make you want to jump out of bed and get going in the morning, a job that drains you, and a job that ultimately makes you feel emotionally defeated. You don't need to stay in that stuck place feeling like you're wearing hobbles and tethered to a post. Sure, making changes can feel overwhelming and hopeless. Once you realize that failing is a part of figuring out your best business, then you'll find yourself moving forward, first at a walk, then a trot, and finally a full out gallop with hair blowing in the wind and joy in your heart. Take baby steps with one small step in front of the next, and, one day soon, you'll be thriving in a business that fills your soul.

3

BLAZE YOUR TRAIL

If you climb in the saddle, be ready for the ride.

o blaze your trail, you have to unhobble your-self and start by putting one foot in front of the other. It simply takes putting the right pieces together with the right timing. It's just like roping a steer. You need to have your rope coiled just right with the hondo sitting in the right spot on your loop. You need to have a ready and willing horse, and you need to have your saddle cinched on tightly. If you break the barrier when the steer jumps out of the shoot, then you get a penalty added onto your time, but you don't stop roping just because you broke the barrier once. It's just like starting a business. You need to have the right resources with the right training and the right people at the right time. It may sound overwhelming or unrealistic, but it's not. It's simply a process to follow regardless of what field you're in, or for what company you work.

The very first step in this process is to identify and clarify your goals. What do you truly want to do? What lights up your spirit? We are going to take an in-depth look at those goals and see if they support your horse passion. Likewise, if your passion supports the goals, then it's far more likely that you will succeed. We will also clarify personal boundaries, which will help you make decisions easier and quicker by being tuned into your gut.

Cowgirls and cowboys have what's called a code. You will be formulating your Cowgirl Code so that you know your boundaries and limits. You want to be prepared to readily respond to a business decision, rather than hastily and emotionally react. Your code will guide you as you negotiate your next steps. This step is all about making a choice to take action or stay where you're at and be content. Whether you are planning to stay in your current job and renegotiate your position, or you are going to transition into owning your own business, the rest of the principles and action steps are the same. Either way, we are going to polish you up so that you know where you're going and how to stand out as the punchy cowgirl that you are.

After creating your code, I will show you how to figure out what business suits you best and how to get it started. I will help you identify your strengths and weaknesses, and gifts, or special talents. As you know, building a business does not happen on its own. I will also help you identify who your followers and promoters will likely be. Hey, you can work as hard as you possibly can, but you need other people for your journey. Team roping is called team because there are two of you. Heck, even with calf roping, you still have your horse as your partner. These people and potential partners need to be identified and relationships intentionally fostered. I'll show you how to do that so that these people keep you on their radar.

Your personal image and how you show up in your business are imperative to solid steady business growth. I will show you how to assess your outer physical image as well as your inner attitude. This cowgirl is not going to pull any punches with you but will shoot straight and tell it like it is. After all, you want and need more money and more time to ride, not another cheerleader fluff book about someone else's journey. You might have to be a big girl and pull up your bootstraps as we navigate your inner and outer appearances. Good luck.

I will spend some additional time on your inner image and attitude because it's simply that important. Your attitude sets the tone and energy for everyone around you, so this piece is particularly important. You will increase your awareness of who you are and finally learn why people treat you the way they do. This is where you will meet your inner cowgirl, that part of you that gets things done, is a leader, and has fun. You will learn how to tap into this part of yourself so that you become the person that people want to do business with and to support.

Most of us have had painful past experiences that we haven't truly processed. We keep telling ourselves the same stupid, painful stories over and over about why things are happening the way they are. Or, we make excuses for ourselves and others that keep us stuck in our miserable place away from our horses. We are going to take those tall tales and set them straight, or in other words, reframe them into stories that will promote your new business into the winner's circle. You'll look at why you have chosen to not follow your passion.

I'm sure you've heard of branding. You're probably thinking of a horse or cattle brand. A cowgirl brands her horse and cattle so when anyone sees that animal, they think straightaway of her. I'm going to show you how to brand yourself. While image plays a part of the brand, the brand is bigger and runs deeper. When you ride for the brand, you work hard, trust, respect, serve, and go the extra mile. You will create your personal brand so that people can look at your work and know that it's yours just by the way it appears, without even having some sort of logo stamped on it. Your brand takes your image and puts it into action. This gives you leadership power.

You will also need to build a team of followers and supporters. Your key players are those in powerful positions that will pull you upward. Your team supports you and uplifts you. You will learn how to build your team and what types of people you need on your team so that they promote you without much effort on your part. This team might even come from places you would not expect.

One thing a cowgirl knows without a doubt is that problems happen. A rope gets hung up. A horse goes to bucking for no apparent reason. The bull gets into the neighbor's herd. Yep, that's how life happens. We are going to look at conflict from your cowgirl perspective and learn how to handle those challenges as you navigate your business. Being a team player adept at conflict resolution rather than a bull in a china shop that simply scares the conflict out of people will propel you forward and save you a lot of wasted time so you can hang out with your horses. You'll learn how a cowgirl handles conflict so that you can take the bull by the horns and escort him right into the trailer and down the road. That's real power and that makes you an indispensable asset in your business.

Keeping yourself motivated and your followers engaged is imperative to the organization and growth of your business. It's part of physics that things move toward chaos. It's called the Law of Entropy. If you don't want your business falling apart, which you don't, then you need to know how to invest in it, keep it organized and engaging, and keep your posse actively supporting you.

Let's talk about obstacles. These are bigger than problems. Problems are a broken fence post that you can easily repair with a new post, a hole digger, some wire, and nippers. An obstacle is much bigger. An obstacle is akin to having to move a herd of heifers across the river and two pastures away, over rough terrain, and all by yourself. Sure, you could probably get it done, but it will cost you a lot of time, energy, and maybe even loss of some of those pricey heifers that you've spent a year doctoring and fattening up. I will show you how to identify those obstacles in your journey and how you can traverse them or avoid them entirely. You will formulate an action plan of next steps so you can quickly implement your advancement process or new business creation.

Most importantly as you navigate these steps, it will serve you to put each one into action before moving onto the next step. If you find yourself pulling back like a young colt on the end of the lead rope, ask yourself what you are afraid of and what is making you balk. Do not accept excuses. Underneath fear is the need to protect yourself from something. Underneath the "I don't know" is usually some knowledge. Dig deeper until you come up with those answers. They are inside you. Don't give up. A cowgirl never does. She dusts off her britches and gets right back in the saddle to try again.

It's time to strap on your spurs and get ready to Cowgirl Up!

4

YOUR COWGIRL CODE

A halo only needs to drop a few inches to become a noose.

Creating your Cowgirl Code is a key piece to anything you do in life, from negotiating a raise to
creating your own business. It's a written state-
ment of who you are and what you will accept. It's your
foundation. It holds your halo up so it doesn't become a
noose. It's that important.

Whether you stay in your current job or start a business, your professionalism shines through in your code.
Consider that every business has, or should have, a mission and values from which they operate. The values

should be relatively stable, but reviewed often to ensure that the company is staying true to itself. The mission is similar, except that it might morph and grow over time as opportunities arise. This is the same for you. You need a solid set of values that you review often, with a mission that will grow as your business grows. Because you are becoming a solopreneur, sometimes it is more difficult to say no to people who might ask for all kinds of concessions, such as a discount, a special deal, or custom work for no charge. Don't skip this section or you will find yourself floating along like tumbleweed in any wind tunnel that pops up, and ultimately letting other people and situations control your life.

I'll first discuss the cowgirl attitude and what that entails. From there, I will explore the components of a Cowgirl Code. Then you will create your Cowgirl Code. Finally, you will decide which trail you will take to earn more money so you can enjoy your horses more.

The cowgirl attitude is one of determination, focus, and drive. She is a woman who presses forward no matter what the circumstances. You don't see cowgirls quit because of a little adversity. She's going to figure out a way through or around the challenge. She certainly doesn't take the challenges personally. She simply knows that challenges are part of life and she can overcome them. Cowgirls don't whine. If you want to Cowgirl Up, then you simply do it.

Cowgirl Up

Cowgirl Up came from the term Cowboy Up. When a cowboy was getting atop the bronc or bull in the bucking shoot, ready to nod for the gate to open, someone would yell "Cowboy Up!" The same thing goes for cowgirls. When a cowgirl is getting seated atop her bronc, ready for the ride to begin, her helper yells "Cowgirl Up," so the gatekeeper and rodeo clowns jump to attention, focusing on the rider. She nods, the gate swings open, and the bronc leaps out of the chute.

Cowgirl Up signifies the courage and grit needed to mount up and ride through the bucks. Sure, she might have some fear, but she puts fear in the back seat and lets the ride roll. The bronc leaps and spins, head between his knees, squalling each time his hooves slam into the ground, yet she moves with grace and ease, poignantly balanced upon his back. She knows how to respond, and how to predict the bronc's next move by paying attention to small things like the quiver of a muscle, twist of the back, and swing of the neck. She's perfectly in the moment and not bothering to worry about all the what ifs because, ultimately, she knows she's in control. She could bail off so the ride stops, but it's the ride that brings the amazing feeling of knowing she did it and that she can do it again. So, when her pickup man comes to help her, she grabs on and dismounts gracefully, letting out a woohoo, a big smile, and laughter that penetrates her soul.

Learning how to Cowgirl Up in your business means planning your action steps, looking ahead so you are prepared for each task, taking action, and working *on* your business and *in* your business. Keeping a pulse on the industry and watching current events is imperative to moving with the changes, rather than being left behind. This will help you to see opportunities for growth. So, let's Cowgirl Up and open the gate so your business journey is finally free.

Cowgirl Code Creation

Your Cowgirl Code is your personal code of conduct. We all need these because sometimes we find ourselves behaving in a manner that makes us ask, "Who was that?" We don't recognize ourselves and wonder from where the outburst erupted, or why we bit our lips and said nothing when we knew something was terribly wrong. Your Cowgirl Code can be a Word document, a pretty Publisher page, or a journal with stickers. However you choose to make it, it should be written down and creatively you. Don't get hung up on the idea that it needs to be some professional document. Let yourself be creative. This is your private piece. It is a reflection of your deepest beliefs.

Your Cowgirl Code should contain the following components: values, goals, moral and ethical beliefs, mental health and physical health statements, and boundaries. You might think this is a bit overboard and has nothing to do with making more money. It has everything to do with that. Your code will help you decide once and for all whether you should stay in your current job and be content or follow your passion into a new business venture.

In all the people that I have coached, there have been quite a few that uncovered pieces of themselves that they forgot existed. If you find that a pay raise is your big goal, then hooray for you because this book will still take you there! Either way, as you write your statements, you will learn why you want what you want and how to stick to your guns so you're not floating around like tumbleweed.

Values

Make a list of your top five values with one being the most important. This could include people, things, pets, attitudes, or feelings. Take some time considering these values. If you're not sure of the order, put them in a different order and see how that fits. Would you die for your number one value? Would you give money to your values? Both of these questions might help you to determine how much you value the item. Don't say you value something just because you think it's the right answer. Nobody is grading you and certainly your boss won't see your list…as long as you keep it off your work computer.

Pay attention to the order of your values because revelations will come from items that are also lower on your list. That's why it's so important to not lie to yourself. Don't do the correct thing; do the *you* thing! If you value something above a relationship, then that should tell you that the relationship isn't really working out for you.

Once you have your values listed, sleep on it. Look at it first thing in the morning and check your initial attitude when you read it. Did your list make you smile? Did you hold your breath? Did something just not feel right in your gut? Change your list. A cowgirl goes with her gut feeling because she's living in the present, not worrying about what the audience thinks. She knows they are sitting outside the arena, not participating in the action.

Here's my list of values:

1. God
2. Family
3. Horses
4. Service
5. Fun

Creating my list didn't happen overnight. It took several days to feel comfortable with it. I've always been spiritual, and when I put God at the top of my list, my life started to make more sense. Life has little meaning to me without family and friends, so that was an easy second. Horses almost tied for second, but my children were the tipping point. Serving others gives me great satisfaction to see them achieve their goals and better their lives. Finally, if life isn't infused with fun and laughter, then it can get pretty draining.

Goals

Simply write down a list of all the things you want to accomplish: make more money, buy a new saddle, fix up the horse trailer, lose 20 pounds, ride on a cattle drive, and whatever else. Anybody that has formally written goals knows that they need to be SMART goals: Specific, Measurable, Achievable, Realistic, and Timely. I like to add in a big scary goal too. It's important to stretch yourself out of your comfort zone. That's paramount to being a cowgirl. No cowgirl I know has ever been happy with the status quo and playing it safe. That's just not the makings of a cowgirl.

Once you have your list of SMART goals written in the order of importance, then let them sit for a day. Review them in the same fashion as you reviewed your values. Are they in the order that feels good? Are they a bit scary?

Put your goals list right next to your values list so that you can see both lists. Is it possible to meld your lists into one? Do your goals reflect your values and vice versa? If you value family and relationships as your number one value, but have your top five goals related to work, then you might need to take a better look at your goals. How much do you really want that job promotion?

Will you be happy working those hours, taking on the stress and responsibility of a career advancement? Are you aware of what the next job rung really entails? You need to be real and raw with yourself. Do you want the job promotion because someone else is pushing you into it? Or because somewhere along your life journey, you were made to believe that until you become the CEO, you haven't really achieved anything.

You need to be certain that these goals are what you want and not what someone else has told you that you want. If deep down they aren't really your goals, then you won't be happy with the job promotion, and you certainly won't perform well. You'll be a disappointment to your colleagues, your Board of Directors, and most importantly, to yourself. When a cowgirl does something that she doesn't fully have faith in, it only ends up biting her.

Several years ago, I travelled with a friend out west. We met up with some other friends in the Badlands and went trail riding. I didn't bring my own horses because I was assured that there would be a broke horse for me to ride. I figured that even if it was a little bit fiery, I could still ride it. Well, the first day I rode a big mule. He seemed friendly enough, but if you don't know about mules, they can be somewhat finicky about who gets on their backs. This mule was a nice one though. For the first part of the cool morning, the trail wound in and out of some really peaceful wooded areas. We rode single file because that's all the trail accommodated. I rode in the back, behind the horses and the pack mule. My mule was easy going and seemed to be a fine partner.

After lunch, I rode in the middle of the pack. My friend, who was not an experienced rider, kept running her horse up on the mule's backside. He was getting angry and would put his big mule head down between his legs, grab the bit in his mouth, and take off running. This was a bit scary because the trail was single file and we were on the edge of a butte with a wall of mountain on one side and an about seven-story drop off on the other. At one of the gate crossings, while we waited for one of the cowboys to shut the gate, my mule heard a nearby creek trickling along and decided that since his back was itchy, he would just lie down right there in the sandy ground and roll. Hello – I was still on his back.

Fast forward to the next day. The cowboy who owned the mule decided that I should ride his horse instead and that he wanted to ride the mule. Here's where I knew better. That horse was all welted up from being chewed on by bugs all night. He had welts the size of flat golf balls. I suggested that maybe we don't use him since he looked so uncomfortable. I wasn't afraid of riding him, but my gut told me that it probably wasn't really a good idea. We didn't have any other horses, so I reluctantly agreed to ride the welted horse so as to not spoil the day and have to sit in camp. We started off on our ride and he was fiery to say the least. He didn't really want to walk, and I had to keep pulling him back. Not only that, he had a smooth snaffle bit in his mouth that did not afford me any real control should he and I have different plans. He seemed to calm down the farther we rode, but I still felt that his back was hurting him from the sweat building up and the saddle rubbing all those welts.

At one point, midday, my friend and another person took off running right past me up a butte. My horse lifted his hip and let out a little kick at the small pack mule that had been following us for hours. I grabbed the reins and made contact with his mouth. He took another step and all heck broke loose! His head went down and back balled up and he threw me so hard to my left side that I heard every bone in my neck crack like an accordion. The ground looked pretty close, and, for a split second, I considered just letting go and diving onto the ground.

That dang inner cowgirl came alive and, somehow, I pulled myself right back onto his back as he turned right. By now, we were on the side of a small butte, so the ground was at a nice little angle. This horse bucked and spun around eight times or so. I kept my body in the hole, the middle of that circle, being careful to not pull his head around so tightly that he fell over and rolled right on top of me down that hill. I guess at some point, he realized I wasn't coming off and he quit bucking, leaving me a bit dazed. I pointed him to the top of the hill and made him work that hind end to climb that hill. The rest of the ride felt like I was riding a time bomb just waiting for an opportunity to find any little thing to blow up and try me again.

Now, the point of that whole story is that I knew better. I knew it was stupid to even saddle that horse up. Sure, I was laughing once back at camp, feeling high from the adrenaline rush and overcoming the challenge, but had I listened to my gut, I would have totally avoided that situation. I could have been terribly hurt, but in the moment, I made the choice to ride because bailing off would probably have gotten me hurt from hitting the ground or catching hooves as I hit the ground. I honored someone else's wishes of me riding this horse that anybody would have known wasn't fit to ride that day. Anybody wasn't there in the camp. I was. I didn't listen to my gut. Don't do that because you will most certainly get yourself into a situation that isn't good for you. I got lucky, really lucky.

Morals and Ethics

Another component of your Cowgirl Code is your morals and ethics. I tie these two together for simplicity. This is foundational in your code. This also sets your boundaries because it is at the basis of your belief system. What we'll do here is make a list of the following beliefs: life, religion, and the treatment of others.

Under life, list what you believe about the value of life. Do you believe in abortion or physician-assisted suicide? We aren't here to argue whether it's right or wrong or justify why you think so. Simply write out the statements as: I believe / do not believe in _____. I'm sure your mind is going 100 miles per hours with all the reasons. I'm not here to judge, so you don't need to justify this to me. If you feel that you do, then I suggest taking a closer look at why you think I need to know your justification. Yes, that may sound harsh, but if you feel the need to justify, then I question, and you should too, why you need to justify your response if it's truly the response that feels good in your gut or if you're just going along with someone else for fear of creating waves. Maybe you're afraid to stand up and say how you really feel because you don't want to be made fun of, mocked, or disowned.

Let's look at why you might fear stating your moral beliefs in the first place. If you fear repercussions from people around you, then those people simply aren't your herd. Your people will support you regardless of whether you have matching beliefs. I believe that going to church every week is very important. I have some very good friends who probably haven't stepped foot in a church in over a year. I don't try to force my beliefs down their throat or shun them because of it. I still love the heck out of them, and they me! This is how you know you've found your herd. So, don't be afraid to share your values and beliefs. You'll know pretty quickly whether these are your people or not. It's better to find out before you waste any more time. This is true for the people you work with and for your potential clients.

Mental and Physical Health

If you take on a job with more responsibility, your boss needs to know that you can physically and mentally handle that before they promote you. Some corporations require an annual physical and mental health check-up. Consider yourself lucky if you work for such a company. If not, go through this exercise. Count the number of days that you called in sick or had to work from home. Count the number of hours you missed due to some kind of doctor appointment. If you missed more than 10% of your scheduled work days, then perhaps seeking a promotion in your current job might not be a wise choice.

Are you currently dealing with a health issue? Do you already see a mental health provider for an unresolved issue? It is certainly important to take care of yourself, so we need to consider whether adding more stress to your life will be in your best interest. If you feel energized when you awaken in the morning, with a clear mind and joyful outlook, then state that. Simply write one-sentence statements about where you are mentally and physically. Again, be completely honest with yourself. Nobody is grading you or looking at your statements.

Maybe you find that you haven't been taking care of yourself very well. If that's the case, then make a committed effort, and make it a goal, to do something to better care for yourself. This might be going to a counselor, a massage therapist, or a chiropractor. The most important thing is to assess how fit you are for the promotion if you were hiring yourself. If you start your own business, then you can take the time you need for your physical and mental health and not feel stressed over that.

Boundaries

The final part of your Cowgirl Code is to make a list of your absolute no's and some statements that you can practice when these situations arise. If you're like most high achieving, caring women I know, you struggle with saying no. You will take on a task that nobody else will do because you see value in most things, but you tend to avoid seeing the costs. So, we need to have a code to guide us on how to feel guilt-free and when to say no, along with some default statements to protect us from overcommitting and getting burnt out. Remember, when you say no to overworking and overcommitting, then you are saying yes to your horses and yourself.

Consider a few scenarios. It's Friday afternoon, 3pm, and everyone is winding down for the three-day weekend. Your boss sends an email asking someone to take home the project overview to proofread and review the financial spreadsheet for errors. The proposal needs to be tidied up and ready to go Tuesday morning by 8am. Jim responds at lightning speed, "Sorry, no can do. Next time." Caleb responds quickly as well, saying, "Sorry I won't have time since I have to do yard work for my elderly parents all weekend." That leaves you.

You didn't respond as quickly so now you feel like you should do it so it gets done. You immediately feel angry. Once again, the others are dodging responsibilities. You've planned a fun weekend trail riding with friends and know that the proposal will take about five hours of time. You could probably find the time, and it might make you look good for a job promotion, so you reluctantly reply back that you'll get it done.

What are you thinking, little britches? You need to say no and honor yourself. It doesn't matter if you're the last one to reply. Pull out one of your statements from your Cowgirl Code that you keep handy in your saddlebag and be done. Set your boundaries, just like the others, and go enjoy your weekend.

So, what are your default statements? They are simply a "no" response, with no justification. Justification shows weakness of boundaries. Let me give you an example of a good reply: *I wish I could help out with this one, as it's very important for the team; however, I have prior commitments*. Period. Stand your ground.

Your boss will probably ask you directly, especially if you've been the one to give in and carry the load for the team in the past. A direct, but kind reply is needed to stand your ground. How about something like, *Bob, I understand that we are all busy this weekend and that I'm usually the high-achieving go-to person. I cannot make a concession this time. Jim or Caleb will need to step up.* Notice that I never use the word "but." I also don't offer to do it next time. Yes, I point out that I'm the high-achiever and that I've made things work in the past. Yes, it's scary.

Redirecting your boss and saying "no" are tough to do. Your boss might feel gobsmacked, but in the end, he will learn that you have boundaries and everyone needs to respect them. Bosses and customers respect someone who has boundaries and can maintain them in a kind, respectful fashion. You don't need to say that you're sorry. A cowgirl only apologizes when she's in the wrong. She doesn't apologize for her boundaries or her well-being. She also doesn't commit to something she knows she will regret, because she'll end up being mad at herself, just like I was after riding that welted horse. Don't do it.

Your list of hard no's and default statements is a list of your personal policies and responses when people push up on those hard no's. You might want three sub-topics such as personal, business, and relationships. A hard no in business statements might be that you do not give discounts. You can state that as Policy

#X: Discounts are not given because this devalues the service. When verbally telling someone you can simply say, "The company policy is that discounts are not given because it devalues the service." Don't be afraid of losing people who want a deal. They probably just want a deal and not necessarily what you have to offer.

For example, in your business, if someone asks for a discount because they say they don't have the money for your program or service, use your code. Instead of feeling bad and flustered and giving in, you can pull out your Cowgirl Code and say, "The business policy is to hold space in the program for people who make a full commitment both financially and energetically with their time. They get the best results and that's what I want for you. So, when you're ready to be fully engaged, let me know and we can get going. Until then, best of luck!" For a worksheet to help you formulate your list of hard no's go to www.CowgirlBusinessSchool.com/hardnos.

After you have compiled your lists of goals, values, morals, dreams, and health statements, you will look at these each morning and night until you have them memorized. You can make an audio of them and listen to your voice stating them while you commute. Do whatever it takes to review them daily for at least three to four weeks. Then review them every few days and before important events. Take out your code when you need a default response to say no. Your Cowgirl Code will help you stick to your guns and ultimately catapult you ahead. To download worksheets that help you move through the creation of your Cowgirl Code, go to www.CowgirlBusinessSchool.com/code.

If fears pop up, thank them for protecting you and ask of what you need to be made aware. Sometimes, your fears will reveal people and situations that aren't conducive to your business growth. Other times, your fears are trying to protect you from pain linked to your past that your subconscious doesn't know is in the past. This is a time to thank yourself for alerting you to the fact that there is potential danger, so you can be alert as you continue down the trail. The more times you keep going and find that there were no hidden monsters, the easier the trail becomes.

Making the Decision

The most important decision to make at this point is whether your job is in alignment with your Cowgirl Code or if starting a business would better serve you. Do you want to promote yourself in your current job, or promote yourself as a business owner?

Draw four boxes on a page, one column being your job and the other your new business. One box in each column is benefits and the other is costs. Fill in each box with everything you can imagine. Some examples for job benefits might include a consistent paycheck, health insurance, and paid vacation. Business benefits might include freedom, following your passion, being your own boss, and the potential for much greater pay. Costs of a job might be an inflexible schedule, no room for growth, a lack of your true calling and passion, and a fixed income. Costs of a business might be start-up costs, no paid vacation, and, initially, doing all jobs, such as accounting and legal. There are many more that can be added, so spend some time figuring out what your personal benefits and costs are.

If your answers are mostly in alignment with your job, then perhaps you could renegotiate your position. If you really want Fridays off, then offer to work four 10-hour days, or two 12-hour days and two eight-hour days. In your renegotiation, ask to restructure your pay so that you get your base pay with a production bonus. You'll feel better about your day off and have the ability to make more money instead of being strapped to a fixed income.

Once you've finished this exercise, look at your boxes and commit to yourself to make the decision to take action to follow whichever path had more benefits and fewer costs. Right now, either commit to getting a raise at your current job or to starting your own business. In either scenario, you'll be happier you made the decision to take action.

By the way, if you said that a cost of starting your own business is that it's scary, then cross that one out. It doesn't count. As John Wayne said, "Courage is being scared to death, but saddling up anyway." And, if you wrote that you don't know how to start your own business, cross that one off too because we will get that figured out in the next chapters.

If you feel that your job is not serving you and won't ever serve you, then decide and commit to finding a new job or better yet to creating a new business. The best way to earn more, work less and live your passion is through creating a new business around your horse passion. We will explore which businesses you can start in the next chapter.

By now you should have your personal Cowgirl Code written, and your final decision made as to which path you will take at this fork in the road. Either way you choose, commit to that choice 150%. Your Cowgirl Code is your foundation so refer to it regularly. Remember that the start is slow, a simple walk, but as you build momentum through action every single day, you will soon find that you're galloping to your heart's content.

NOD, GATE, AND RIDE

*You have to have your gut and your wisdom
in check before you nod your head.
Freedom comes at the nod of the head
and the swing of the gate.*

R ecently, I sat watching some cowboys riding some bucking bulls, or trying to ride and getting bucked off. As I sat outside the arena in the stands, I watched as each cowboy mounted his bull in the chute, prepared his rigging, adjusted his seat, tucked his chin, and gave the nod. The gate swung open and the bull exploded out of the chute into a tyrant of flying hooves, twisting horns, loud grunts, and clouds of dust. I twisted and lurched with each buck, holding my breath as each cowboy attempted his ride. I cheered wildly when he stayed on for the full eight seconds, and the rodeo clowns intervened to attend to the bull as the cowboy half dismounted and half bucked off. I sat quietly, eyes fixed on the cowboys who got bucked off, waiting for each one to get back on his feet and walk away. When I left the rodeo, I was filled with a renewed excitement and enthusiasm to get myself into the arena. I didn't even care whether I was showing a pleasure horse, running poles or barrels, or team roping. Just let me into an arena where I can get into the game and feel the heart pounding excitement of giving my all and competing against myself to do my next personal best.

Now you're probably wondering what in the world does my rodeo adventure have to do with business building? Well, it has a lot to do with it. Being in the business arena is exactly where you want to be, and in fact, need to be in order to live your passion and build a business. You can't be both inside the arena taking action and at the same time sitting in the stands being a spectator. Plain and simple, if you're not moving, then you're not in the game. You're sitting outside the arena. The longer you sit outside the arena, the more likely you'll stay there. So, let's identify where exactly is your arena, who is in there with you, who is watching from the outside, and who are the supporters.

To identify your exact arena, first look at your strengths, weaknesses, and gifts or talents. I like using a strengths assessment that is scientifically based and well-tested because many times it is difficult to identify our strengths and gifts because those are the things that come easy to us. We figure those things are easy for everyone, so we don't necessarily think of them as strengths. Asking friends what they see in us is also a good way to identify strengths. Many times, we know our own weaknesses because they are things we struggle with and don't care to do. For some people that might be public speaking and making videos. Others might not like writing, or drawing, or physical work. To identify gifts, I like using a spiritual gifts assessment. There are several available that help you identify your God-given talents that are innately you. Some people call it how they're wired. Whatever you want to call it, they are ways that come naturally to serve others.

Choosing a Business

Once you have a list of your strengths, weaknesses, and gifts, let's look at things you could do to start a business. The equine field is wide open. If you like computer work, you can create websites, offer bookkeeping services for horse owners, create graphics and ads, or manage social media for horse businesses. If you like photography, you can do photo shoots at farms or equine events. If you like working at shows, you can do braiding or banding, stall cleaning, lunging, or grooming. Anything you do at a horse show is something you can start a business around.

You can also sell products. Either find a product that someone else makes and sell it or make your own. If you like sewing, make show clothes. You can make jewelry and sell it at shows and online. Or, make chaps, wild rags, or home décor from old lariats. You can make homemade liniments or poultices or make custom tails. You can make fancy picture frames. The list is endless.

You can provide a service. Some examples are graphic design, logo creation, tailoring show clothes, cinch making, leather crafting, banding and braiding, selling feed and supplements, or trailer cleaning and repair. You can clean saddles, repair saddles, or dye saddles. If you like beading and crystalizing, then contact clothing seamstresses and offer your crystal services. There are hundreds of things you can do. What do you need for your horses that you wish you had? What do you love to do that you could also do for others? What do you find yourself doing and losing total track of time when you're doing it?

Choose one thing that you feel comfortable doing that excites you and then identify three sources of income around that business. For example, if you want to dye leather, then dye saddles, dye showmanship boots, and dye chaps. The reason you want to identify three sources is to test your advertising and find out which source has a greater need. Or, maybe you want to do all three sources. This is all about market research and honing in on your market. You can always expand your services, and probably will, once your business is up and running. This step will take some brainpower and research. Use Google and YouTube to get ideas, searching for things you love.

Your People

Another consideration is your following. It's important to identify who your arena spectators are and where to find them. Do you spend most of your time around married trail riders? Do you go to rodeos and run barrels every weekend? Do you hang out with Quarter Horse people, Paint people, or Arabian people? Do you love the racetracks? Who are you friends with on Facebook, Instagram, and LinkedIn? Who do you follow? Who can you help, and how can you help them?

Consider all the people you know. Some are sitting outside the arena watching you. Your spectators can be those who want to be like you, like most spectators are. They can also be people who are looking for their next superstar, their next winner that they can team up with and promote, as well as use to promote their product. There are people scouting about for their next superstar. If you're not in the arena, then they can't find you.

Once you have a business idea, it's time to give the nod and let that gate swing wide open. Survey your friends and family. Announce to your horse friends that you're going to start a business and ask them to rate your ideas. Ask your friends who they would go to for the service or product you're planning to promote.

Use Google, Facebook, YouTube, and Amazon to search for your service or product. Research your competitors and find out where they advertise and what they offer. Make a spreadsheet with services, costs, places they advertise, additional services offered, return policies, and anything else that applies to your business idea. When you decide to build a business, this is the perfect time to identify your competition, your supporters, and your resources.

For very little money, I helped my daughter get started in a business that allows her to have complete control over her schedule so she can go to horse shows. She can also make money while she's at shows. She works on horses, humans, and other animals as a pulsed electromagnetic frequency practitioner, helping them heal quicker so they can perform better. You can check her out at EMF Pro Sport on Facebook.

Before launching her business, she knew that she wanted the flexibility to work at home and at horse shows. She researched what she could do to work on horses. She looked at equine massage, pulsed electromagnetic frequency, laser therapy, and red light therapy.

She looked at required training, initial investment, and ongoing costs. When she chose pulsed electromagnetic therapy, she casually surveyed her friends, searched other practitioners online, and reviewed their websites and Facebook pages. I helped her write goals and choose a company name. Then, she took action by creating awareness through Facebook, talking to friends, and asking others to promote her. Her business is now growing and doing well.

Your Supporters

Let's talk about the guys standing around the bucking chutes helping the cowboys get on their bulls. These guys are very important and can make or break a cowboy's ride. They coach the cowboy, make sure his rigging is on correctly, make sure he's on and ready, and keep him safe should the bull explode in the chute. If the bull decides to explode in the chute, one of these guys will yank that cowboy off the bull so he doesn't get hurt. Who might support you in your new journey? What would they be willing to do for you?

Your chute help can be somebody who might be willing to train you, mentor you, or even partner with you until you're up and running. Find someone that you admire and ask them. The worst that will happen is they say no, and they will still be flattered that you asked. I ask my chap maker each time I see him to teach me how to make chaps the way he does, and each time he laughs and says no. I'm serious, and he knows it. He's flattered, but he does not want the competition. Either way, I'm still alive, and the rejection didn't sting. So just ask.

You also need to identify your clowns and pickup men. The pickup man swiftly rides up next to the bucking bronc and the cowboy grabs onto the pickup man so he can dismount safely. Your clowns are your protectors and keep you safe along with your pickup men, clowns in the bull arena and pickup men in the bronc arena. These guys will jump in front of a bull to make sure you're safe. They'll jump in should a cowboy get his hand caught up in the rigging. They will do anything to keep that cowboy safe. They are honest and reliable and, most importantly, will take a beating to make sure you can ride again.

You might find these people within your industry, or in a related industry. They might be your peer. If you're creating websites, they might be logo creators. If you're selling feed, they could be supplement sales people. Either way, these people are willing to not only help you launch yourself, but they are in the arena with you along for your ride.

So how do you find your protector? Consider the following. Who takes an interest in you? Who asks how you're doing? Who checks in on you, not to see what you've accomplished or to tell you what you need to improve, but to give you a word of encouragement or compliment you? This relationship should be nurtured in a professional manner. Befriend this person professionally. That means that you initiate small conversations. Keep everything positive; do not complain about anything. Share your desire to launch a new business. Let them know you value them and their opinion. This person will easily become your protector and have your back if you let them. These people are naturally supportive, and usually natural networkers. If you let them know you want to get promoted and are starting a new business, they will probably spread the word to the right people who can help you.

It's now time to nod so the gate swings open and you can get into the arena. Making the commitment is the first step to swinging your leg over your bull. Decide right now that you're starting a new business. Clarity and action are the keys to success. Making a choice and putting it into action is the first step. You'll never know if you're on the right trail if you don't trot down the trail and see where it goes. No trail is straight and no business creation is either. Make the commitment to yourself to give it your all. Don't worry about failing. Failures are simply adjustments to your direction as you go.

As you find yourself sitting on your bull in the bucking chute, you'll have your helpers on one side, and the gateman on the other. Your gateman is also very important because he swings the gate open just at the right time.

That right time is when you tell him to, when you nod your head. He needs to be paying attention, focused on you. He needs to open the gate exactly when you nod, not before you're ready or after you've expected it. Remember, your gateman isn't going to open the gate until you nod. You have to nod. You have to make the commitment and take action in order to get out into the playing field.

If you're not nodding, then what's keeping you from doing so? You don't have to have a new completed business plan. You don't have to have your new business service or product finished and set in stone before you start calling people. You must, however, make the first call. Pick up your phone and call your friends and prospects. This is what gets you into the arena where you're in the game.

Now not every cowgirl wins the class, let alone wins the class on her first ride. It's not likely she'll have the fastest time around the barrels on her very first go. You know that, so don't be afraid of what you already know. Every time you ride, it gives you a chance to practice what you've learned just a little more. Just like in business, every call you make gives you another chance to practice how you approach your prospect. Don't be pushy; do it from a place of a serving heart. The point is that you have to take the first step and do it.

Remember there are spectators watching and scouting, and your chute help is also there. If people are not supportive, or, worse yet, are mocking, then maybe it's time to consider if this is the arena for you. There are many, many arenas to play in. It's your choice which one you want to be in.

Now let's say you've found supportive chute help to get you on your bull, tighten your rigging, and keep you safe. And you've got a gateman focused on you waiting for the nod. Are you nodding? Ever? Have you made it known that you're ready to get in the game? Have you told the world what you are doing by creating awareness of your new business through online posts and pictures, flyers, and personal conversations? They might all be staring at you and all you're doing is sitting on the bull, afraid to nod because deep down you're afraid to put yourself out into that arena, afraid to tell people about your new business. The chute feels safe. After all, you might get bucked off and laughed at, or hear that they thought you couldn't do it anyway.

Well, cowgirls don't worry about those things. Do you know why? It's because you are focused on what you are doing, not looking out at the spectators worrying about what kind of applause, or lack thereof, you might get. This is a very important point, so I'm going to grill it into you again. If you are focused on the bull you are riding (the project, job, or business you are getting ready to do), and you have committed to giving it your all, then you can't also be worrying about what somebody is going to say or do in the future. Your passion and fear cannot co-exist if you are 100% engaged. It's one or the other. So, choose passion. Acknowledge your fear, thanking it for trying to keep you safe by playing small, and then say goodbye. Life is not truly lived in the backseat, or in the chute. So, make the nod and get into the arena so you can get into the game. The right people will see you and want to play in your arena too.

Some of you might feel like you're already in the game and still not getting your business launched. You're frustrated that you are doing a lot of work, showing up day in and day out. I challenge you that you're not actually in the game. You might be doing busy work, organizing stuff, and pretending to launch your business. The only way to truly launch a business is to make sales. If you're not selling your product or your service, then you're not launching and you're still hanging out in the chute.

If you're not making sales, then consider why. First, tell people what you're doing and create awareness that you exist. Promote yourself. Sell yourself. Share what you're doing every chance you get. If you're not, then what's holding you back? What are you afraid of? Are you afraid you might look stupid? Or say the wrong thing? Or sound fake? Stop making excuses and allowing distractions to pull you away. The initial sales are the toughest. Consider how you can help others solve their problems with your service or product, and you won't feel like you're selling.

If asking for payment makes you uncomfortable then think of money as another form of energy. Your clients must give up something to get what you have. Money is the easiest thing to give you in exchange for what you have. Simply asking how your client wants to pay for the item is how to close a sale. After you've shared how you can help them with what they need, say, "I take PayPal or credit cards (or whatever you take). Which would you like to use today?" You've given them a clear choice and told them when to make the decision, so there shouldn't be any confusion.

If they balk or argue, then I give one chance to see if there's something holding them back that can be resolved. I ask, "What is holding you back, and if that block did not exist, then what would you do?" If they are stalling or arguing and not wanting to solve their problem, then I don't make it any more uncomfortable for them and I sweetly tell them that maybe this isn't for them right now. End your conversation with best of luck or talk to you soon or whatever. Don't waste any more time on someone that isn't ready for you or that wants your time, energy, talent, and products for free. You are worth far more!

Cowgirl Power

Cowgirl Power is about having the confidence to stand up for yourself and to do the right thing. It is about having healthy boundaries and the ability to say no without getting angry or justifying your answer. It is having a large, positive presence so that people know you are there without you having to say much. It is the energy you emit when you're in a group of people. So how does one suddenly stand up and have power?

Power can be nurtured and grown. The first step is to increase your self-awareness and how you show up to the game. Are you complaining and seeing all the problems? Are the problems obstacles that are insurmountable? Do you enter a room with a scowl or frown? Maybe you are the person who always seems happy and helpful, but underneath the sweet exterior you are grumbling to yourself. People can feel that energy. So, the first step is to observe yourself and how you approach other people. Once you become aware of your attitude, then look at your actions. Actions follow attitude. So, do you get angry right away? Or, is your default to shrivel up and feel overwhelmed? Maybe you love challenges and jump in head first but soon get burnt out. Power is about being aware of your reactions and instead choosing your response. When I've coached my daughters before they ride into the show pen, I always tell them to show like they own the arena and have already won. Having that attitude has put us in the winner's circle more than having a great horse.

We will dive deeper into power in the next few chapters as we examine attitudes and image. For now, picture yourself as the calm, intelligent cowgirl who is aware of her surroundings and her people at all times.

Just a few housekeeping things you should consider. Always ask your legal advisor and accountant for information on how to structure your business entity. Starting out as a sole proprietorship is the easiest. To open a bank account, you will probably need a business license that you can obtain from your county or city government office. Keeping a simple spreadsheet is a good way to track your money coming in and expenses going out. Make sure you are paying your taxes so you don't get fined. Again, ask your accountant.

COWGIRL ATTITUDE

A word to the wise is unnecessary.

Perhaps the most important part of building a business is how you show up to other people, specifically your posse. Your image precedes your reputation. Your image is what people see and feel within the first 30 seconds of meeting you. You already know that. I'm simply reminding you because so many times we tend to forget the importance of image, or we simply feel defeated from life's blows, so we become bitter and lazy. I'm going to challenge you to not only consider your outer image, but also the attitudinal image that you're projecting.

First consider your physical image. From a cowgirl's standpoint, you need to be outfitted in gear that you can comfortably wear while working. A cowgirl also pays attention to detail and wants to look good. Her shirt is pressed, and her jeans are clean. If she's going to be anywhere but in the saddle on the open range, her jeans will be creased and starched. Her hat is creased, and she's wearing a wild rag (a neck scarf) that not only looks good but also does its job of protecting her from wind, sun, and blowing dust.

You, as a business woman, need to do the same. I shouldn't have to say the following, but my experience is that I need to say some basics here. Your clothes need to be clean – always. Your hair needs to have a comb through it, at least every morning. Yes, I've seen some women who think that running their fingers through their hair and pulling it into some kind of messy bun is acceptable. It's not acceptable if you want to build a business.

I know some of you are thinking that the business world has loosened its standards. Sure, they have, but not necessarily by choice. More so because that's simply how people are showing up. Women aren't combing their hair. They have tattoos peeking out from under their shirts or around their ankles. Cleavage is falling out of tight shirts. If I'm looking to hire and promote someone, I notice those very things, and so do customers and prospective clients. It's simply not professional. Of course, it's your choice to present yourself in that manner, but what it tells others, and me, is that you don't pay attention to detail, and you're a bit of a rogue. It makes me wonder how likely you are to perform a thorough, mistake-free job and if you're even open to suggestions and feedback.

One can argue that the rogue, wild-spirited attitude is also the creative person, but I say that you can be a creative problem-solver with a professional appearance. If my spending money is on the line, I'm banking on the person who shows up in clean, pressed clothes, hair washed and brushed, and no tattoos or cleavage hanging out. I want to feel like the person I'm hiring is professional, even if they are cleaning a stall.

Please understand that I'm not saying that tattoos are bad. I've seen some amazing tattoos that are truly works of art. However, in the equine industry you won't find those tattoos. People are generally conservative regarding tattoos. The horse people who have tattoos usually only have small ones that are easily hidden. Yes, this is a generality. You can always find horse lovers with full sleeve tattoos. However, you will likely find more people who have no tattoos or small ones that are covered. The point is that it's best for the business person to show up like the people they are serving. If you want to serve people with large, colorful tattoos then yes, definitely show yours! It will be a great ice breaker! While I believe we should be authentic instead of playing it safe, just remember that *in general* horse people will be conservative with their tattoos.

Another point for women to consider is what message they want to send to those around them. Wearing a partially see-through blouse with several buttons unbuttoned so I can see your under-garments tells me you don't have healthy boundaries. Sure, that attire and your cleavage is perfectly fine if you're going out on the town, but in a business setting I won't be promoting you if every time I look at you, I see 6" of cleavage. This goes the same for skirt and shorts lengths. It isn't classy if you bend over and your booty can be seen.

Finally, whatever you wear, make sure it fits appropriately. That means that it's not skin-tight. Unless you're built like a model and are 5'9" and 125 pounds, skintight clothing simply is not flattering. Your clothing can fit well without showing every bulge and curve. Buying a bigger size that fits better gives a classier appearance and helps you stand out as a professional business woman. While image may seem trivial to some, it's not to your potential clients. They want to know that they can be proud of the person they've hired and not hold their breath wondering what clothing you're going to don today.

As I mentioned before, people judge your appearance within the first 30 seconds, or less, upon meeting or even seeing you. Let's not start out at a disadvantage. Remember the following basic guidelines:

1. Comb your hair
2. Wear well-fitting, not tight-fitting, clothing that is not low-cut, too short or see-through.
3. Make sure your clothes are clean, pressed, and smell fresh.
4. Cover tattoos, if appropriate.

Attitude

Your attitude is also paramount to your image. People can read your attitude by how you carry yourself, your tone of voice, and your facial expressions and body language. We all know that if someone is frowning, then they have a negative attitude. Do you know what your body is saying about your attitude? Have you ever seen how you look walking into an interview or board meeting to discuss your promotion? How you show up is your choice, but first you must be aware of those small nuances you're projecting that reflect your underlying attitude.

I have outlined several attitudinal syndromes that you might be choosing without even realizing it. These syndromes are ways that we show up with little awareness. There are five negative syndromes that I'll describe. See if you can identify yourself in any of these syndromes. Think back to a time when you were stressed over something and see if you reacted with one of the following syndromes. Many times when we react, we have a default syndrome that we have chosen over and over without even realizing we are making the choice. Sometimes we have a bit of a realization, but we justify our actions because we don't want to consider that we actually have a choice in how we control our behavior and attitude. Some of those excuses are:

- That's just how I'm wired.
- He makes me so mad, or he drives me crazy, or he….
- I can't help it.
- I don't know what to do.
- My feelings aren't wrong.
- I just don't know.

While all of the above sound reasonable, they are simply excuses to justify your behavior and demonstrate a lack of self-control. Cowgirls don't blame others, nor do they make excuses for their weaknesses. They Cowgirl Up. They mount up, nod for the gate to open, and ride their hearts out. Excuses don't get the job done, the career advanced, or the business promoted.

Packhorse Syndrome

The first syndrome is the Packhorse Syndrome. I'm being nice by calling it a packhorse, but in reality, we usually use pack mules. They wear a special rig that holds large canvas packs on both sides of their bodies, evenly balanced and strapped on. Many times, there are several mules. They walk single file, tied onto the mule in front of them, with the head mule being led by a rider. His or her whole job is to carry the load for everyone. How many times have you felt like you're carrying the load? You're doing everything from working your job, starting your business, managing the home, cleaning the barn, buying the groceries, and remembering everybody's birthdays.

The cowboy or cowgirl leading the pack mules have to pay attention to their rigging so that it doesn't slip off. He also has to ensure that none of the pack mules go lame because a sore pack mule isn't any good. He can't carry the load. They carry the supplies for the group and help get the job done. However, the pack mules usually stay as pack mules. They don't suddenly go from being a pack mule or packhorse to a roping horse that gets to ride the plains chasing wild cows, or team rope in the arena. The pack mules don't become the superstars. Yes, they're needed, but they are needed as pack mules, supply transporters, helpers.

You might find that this is where you operate within your company and your life. You do a ton of work. You get an accolade here and there, but you're kept in your spot. Eventually you burn out, show up lame, and simply don't want to do anything more. The important thing to do is to be aware of whether or not you participate in this syndrome. If you do, then making the choice to set boundaries and move away from being the pack mule is what you need to do to launch a business and get promoted. I'll address how after I discuss the other syndromes.

School Horse Syndrome

Another syndrome is the School Horse Syndrome. This is similar to the pack mule in that you do the brunt of the busy work. However, everybody loves the school horse because he's available and anybody can ride the school horse without getting hurt. He is safe and reliable. The school horse loves the attention he gets from all the different people who ride him. However, the school horse runs in circles in the arena all day teaching his riders new skills and making them look accomplished. Once the riders are finished with their lessons, they give him a quick pat and put him away. They simply tie the school horse back up in his stall and leave. He doesn't really belong to any one rider. He doesn't get to ride the trails or the open range. He doesn't have a special partner and he never really goes anywhere. Life is mundane for him, but at least he gets some positive attention every now and then, when someone needs him, unlike the pack mule that follows the mule in front of him, nose to hind end.

Sometimes I see businesswomen with the School Horse Syndrome. They run in circles making others look good and promoting others, but they themselves never get their businesses launched or promoted. Eventually the school horses get worn out and develop bad habits. Then they either get beaten until they behave or sold down the road. The business woman might get short tempered, sloppy with details, or have shut down communication leading to constant reprimands and rarely a kind or encouraging word, or worst-case scenario, her business fails. She has spent a long-time helping others, teaching others, giving away her time and talents, and running in circles, only to remain invisible to her clients.

The Gunslinger Syndrome

The Gunslinger Syndrome is possibly the most common syndrome in corporate America. With this syndrome, the person shows up with guns a-blazin'! She is ready for a gunfight and will jump at the chance to win that fight at all costs. She has an *I win you lose* attitude towards solving problems and completing tasks. This person scowls a lot and uses fear and intimidation to get what she wants. Sometimes, it even works. It's her way or the highway. This type of person can initially be confused for a go-getter, but after a few outbursts with guns drawn, she is easily identified. You might find yourself walking on eggshells around this person, tiptoeing past her office door, or hiding in your office to avoid her as much as possible.

This attitude is not one of a true leader. She'll also be sure to take credit for everything and give very little to where it's due. Her default reaction to anything is one of anger. How many times have you gotten mad when things didn't go your way? How often do you have to be right? How often do you feel slighted because someone else got something you wanted and so you vowed to stop interacting with him or her? You might have Gunslinger Syndrome.

Round Pen Syndrome

The Round Pen Syndrome is also fairly common. With this syndrome, you find yourself running in circles, or spinning your wheels. You work hard, again, doing busy work. You make excuses for other people. You tolerate a lot. When someone dumps a load of work on you, you might hear yourself saying, "Well he has a lot to do this weekend with his family. I'll do the project." Or to the chronically late person, you might say, "You drive from such a distance. That traffic must be horrible. Let me know when you're going to be late, and I'll meet you at 2AM to get your horse's tail braided." Sure, those are nice things to do, but you do them all the time and never get fairly compensated. I'm not saying that you need to be inflexible, but you also don't need to make excuses for other people's actions. You play it safe by being super busy in your little corral, rather than playing it big on the open range.

You are building a business. You need to look like a leader with integrity and the best candidate to solve the problems of your followers. While it is admirable to help others and be a team player, there is a difference between helping someone solve their problem and enabling them to continue to take advantage of others. You want to shine like the superstar that you are. You don't want to make excuses for yourself or anyone else. On the flip side, you really don't want to criticize others or bring their faults to the sharing table. Starting a business is about you winning without stepping all over other people. Let them step on themselves.

Boss Mare Syndrome

Let's talk about one last syndrome: Boss Mare Syndrome. This is another great syndrome that many women choose. You like to be in control and organize the team. You like calling the shots. You also like taking care of people, so you'll help people a lot by giving them your opinion and ideas. You are comfortable calling the shots. You're just like the alpha mare in the herd. She's the top dog, bossing everyone else around. She gets to the feeder first and eats what she wants, rotating to other feeding spots and pushing the other horses away as she sees fit.

She leads the herd. When she goes out to pasture, the others fall into line and follow her. When she heads to the water trough, the others make their way to the trough for a sip of fresh water after she's had her fill. If she senses danger with ears pointed forward, eyes gazing at the horizon, and every muscle on high alert waiting to flee, all the other horses watch her, ready to bolt also.

If you perform in your job like the Boss Mare, then you most certainly feel like you're building a great business. After all, you're already leading your followers. You call the shots and get the job done. You're not like the Gunslinger, using fear and intimidation. The downfall here is that your followers are simply following. You're not building a great team. You have followers because you're a strong, caring person, but *you* still have to do the brunt of the work. Eventually, you'll get burnt out because you're always the one calling the shots, and your team is mindlessly following.

Your team is not really engaged, not really supporting you, and they certainly aren't promoting you. You can't figure out why. It's because you're overbearing, and while you help them and get the job done, plainly put, you're bossy. When you get burnt out, you become the Gunslinger. You bare your teeth. Hooves fly as you stomp out of an office or meeting. You have a difficult time apologizing because you feel as if you've been giving great ideas and the team just doesn't step up to the plate.

Identifying which syndromes you choose and learning how to choose a better syndrome are very important to developing yourself into a business woman. All of the syndromes described stem from underlying negative or self-destructive attitudes. It is difficult to identify your own syndromes because if it were easy, you probably wouldn't be choosing them.

One way to increase your awareness around your syndromes is to look at how you react when something does not go as planned. When you didn't make the sale, how did you react right at the time you were first told no? Were you angry? Did you secretly want to slash the tires of the person who rejected your offer? Did you take a deep breath, sigh, and feel like you just need to work harder? Did you make excuses for why they talked to you for an hour and then said no thank you? Did you decide that you would just work harder and put your nose to the grindstone only to later decide that it's not really worth it because you've been working hard for a while already?

Once you become aware of how you react to stressful situations, you'll be better able to choose how you want to respond. What is most important is that you understand that you can choose which syndromes you want to use and when. Sometimes the Gunslinger motivates a lazy client into action. They need to hear a few firecrackers! However, I don't suggest choosing these syndromes since they are based off of negative attitudes, and you generally do not get sustained positive results from negative attitudes. You might get short-term results from motivating with fear or from manipulation, but nothing will last. Your followers won't see you as a positive driving force in solving their problems, so you probably won't be hired again.

Remembering that you have the power to choose your own syndrome can help you in your business. I recently presented a high-end program to a client. He immediately wanted to know what would happen if he didn't get the results that I proposed. He demanded to see the "fine print" so he could be protected when the program didn't work. I quickly identified him as a Gunslinger. He was trying to push my buttons and start a fight.

Instead of drawing my guns and engaging in a heated argument, I chose a positive and curious response, asking what he thought would not work. He couldn't answer the question and continued to demand to see the refund policy. Realizing that he wanted a fight, I then chose to set a boundary and told him that the program could certainly fail since I can't be with him every minute to oversee his engagement and because he was looking for the failure and not the goal, he would not be a good fit for the program. As soon as I took it away, he changed his attitude and signed up for the program, paying in full that night. It sounds like magic, but it's simply identifying and choosing attitudes.

In the next chapter, I'll show you some positive syndromes that will reap you better, longer-lasting results building your business stronger and faster.

7

MEET YOUR INNER COWGIRL

*It ain't the clothes that make the cowgirl,
it's the attitude and heart.*

ello, cowgirl! That's right. Inside of you is an inner cowgirl, a wild and free spirit longing to let go of all the negative feelings and heavy stuff cluttering your mind, someone who doesn't fear what others think of you or how they judge you. There's an inner cowgirl inside you who is confident, intelligent, and poised. She is aware and tuned into her gut feelings. She knows when something doesn't feel right and knows how to tackle the issues at hand in a way that works for everyone involved. She isn't afraid to speak her mind but does so in a respectful and kind manner. It's about time you meet your inner cowgirl.

Your inner cowgirl is strong and passionate. She knows what she likes and what she doesn't like. She knows how to say no without feeling guilty. She leads with grit and integrity. She has Cowgirl Power, a power that flows freely from her spirit, driving her with intention and awareness. She is confident and focused on her task at hand, while also considering her past and future. She looks back without regret, but instead to learn so that she can process the old and release any hold it tries to have on her. She looks forward with insight so that she is aware of her trail, foreseeing any obstacles. She knows when to ask for help and where her limits lie. Your inner cowgirl will help you choose your right business, build and nurture it, and get promoted when you listen to the whisperings she shares with you.

Cowgirl Strong Syndrome

There are two primary syndromes that make your inner cowgirl shine. The first I call Cowgirl Strong Syndrome. You are aware of who you are, and you trust yourself to do the best you can do at any time with the resources that you have. You see challenges as a regular part of life. In fact, you welcome challenges because they are an opportunity to grow. You look at the challenge as if it's a puzzle to be solved. You hold the challenge in your hands, feel it, turn it over, open it up, and examine it. You formulate a solution that is a win for all involved, and most importantly, you spring into action. If the solution doesn't work for all parties, you simply look for a new and better solution. Taking action is key to being a cowgirl. You don't quit, or whine that it's too hard or not fair. You cut your losses and move on, all the while trusting that your journey is the one where you are supposed to be. If you feel stuck, you simply sit in that place of stuckness, being aware of everything around you, trusting that the answer will appear when you're ready.

Rodeo Bronc Syndrome

The second syndrome is the Rodeo Bronc Syndrome. It's not really fair to call it a syndrome; a ride sounds more appropriate. This is when you're out in the limelight of the arena, running your business with total ease and confidence. Your passion is shining through. You feel as if you were made to do what you're doing. You feel like everything is fun and easy. If you were a cowgirl, you'd be riding the bronc, anticipating his every move, in total synch with his body, hanging on and spurring for him to buck harder because you know you can ride through the bucks. You beat his hooves to the ground. What I mean by that is you are so aware and intuitive that you know when and where his hooves will hit the ground with each buck that you are able to anticipate the hooves hitting the ground and ride right through the jolt and into the next explosive leap. Your intuition is on fire! Time isn't counting down on the eight-second timer because time doesn't even matter. You're riding to express your passion and the spirit that flows within you. You aren't out there to impress anyone. You're doing what you love, and others will see that and cheer you to victory.

Sure, this might seem like unicorns and ice cream cones, and you might be wondering how on God's green earth does this remotely apply to the business world. Let me share a scenario of how your inner cowgirl can help you get your business promoted. You've already made six sales calls and haven't had one person interested in your service. You're feeling angry, and it's getting more difficult to pick up the phone and call another person. Sales calls are not a fun task, especially first thing Monday morning. In fact, when your alarm rings out in the morning, you find yourself hitting the snooze button more often than not. You're still showing up to work your business, but you're not smiling as much, and you certainly don't feel as motivated anymore. If you were calling yourself, I'm pretty sure you wouldn't consider buying anything from your call or helping promote your business. Your potential clients might be wondering why your attitude lacks energy and excitement. You appear to have chosen a negative attitude and it shows in your words and actions. Your clients aren't interested in investing time or energy into someone who is an energetic drain on them. They probably wonder if you'll perform a good, thorough job. You need to change your attitude from a negative syndrome to a positive syndrome. You need to stop acting like the lame packhorse and choose something that will appeal to your prospective clients so that your clients buy from you and feel confident to promote you to others.

So how do you suddenly change from the Packhorse Syndrome to the Cowgirl Strong Syndrome? At the most basic level, it's a choice. It's not an easy choice though. First, as I've said before, you have to identify that you're even choosing the Packhorse Syndrome, or whatever negative syndrome you've chosen. Then, you have to consciously decide to choose another syndrome. This takes energy and intention. It generally takes 21 days to form a new habit, but I recently heard it takes 66 days to form a new *positive* habit. That makes sense. Forming positive habits takes more energy. It's a lot easier to fall into the bad habit of letting your horse walk off when you mount than making him stand patiently waiting for your cue. In business, it's easy to waste time on social media (bad habit) instead of making phone calls (good habit). The first step to forming a positive habit begins the minute you awaken. Every day when you wake up, before your feet hit the floor, stop and state your intentions, pray, meditate, or whatever you call it. Once you have spent that time being intentional about how you're going to behave, think, and feel for the day, then jump out of bed and into your morning routine.

What happens when the challenges arise? You have the opportunity to choose your response and test yourself. See how well you adhered to your intentions that you set in the morning. If you totally flew off the handle and showed up guns a-blazin', then at least be aware that you chose the Gunslinger Syndrome. You'll most certainly have more opportunities to practice how you want to respond to challenges because I guarantee more will come your way. The universe has a way of continuing to challenge us with the same challenge wrapped up in different people and different locations until we master our positive response. Regardless of what your initial response is to a challenging situation, you can stop yourself and immediately choose a different syndrome. Sure, some people around you will wonder what came over you and why the sudden change in attitude, but a cowgirl doesn't worry about being judged or having to rationalize or justify her behavior. She simply focuses on solving the problem and moving on to the next pasture and gate to walk through, or the next bronc she will ride.

Choosing the positive syndrome is tricky for certain. It takes consciously planning your day and knowing that challenges will sneak up and trip you from behind or cow kick you from the side. Being aware of your surroundings will help, but sometimes we can't even begin to predict the rug being snatched out from under our feet. All we can do is take a deep breath while we choose our response.

Let's go back to the scenario of being rejected for the sale. Sure, you were frustrated in the moment when you spent an hour telling the potential client how you could help him, and then he said no and hung up. Did he not even have the decency to tell you that he wasn't interested before you spent an hour's time sharing your plan? No. He gladly took your plan and walked away. You're angry to your core and ready to take the bull by its horns. I can tell you that's a really bad idea because that bull will probably gore you. Take a deep breath and reframe this situation so that you can look at it from another perspective. Step into your prospect's boots. Be curious about why he didn't buy your service. How possible is it that he might want to share your information with his friend who owns 16 racehorses? If you respond negatively now, then you might just change his mind and lose the opportunity to get a much larger sale. Maybe your prospect simply took your plan and is going to implement it on his own. This is the perfect time to take a personal inventory and consider what you said on the call and why he didn't buy from you.

Personal Inventory

When you take a personal inventory, you step out-side of your angry self and into your inner cowgirl. If you need help with that, pretend that you're taking off any ugly outfit that you hate and putting on a really punchy outfit that you love. Then read the description of your inner cowgirl at the beginning of the chapter. Now, consider the following on a scale of 0 to10 with 0 being completely non-existent, and 10 being amazing:

- What skills do you have that make you shine?
  - How comfortable are you speaking in front of a crowd?
  - How organized are you in processes?
  - How creative are you in formulating solutions?
  - How friendly are you in a group?
  - How successful are you with sales?
- How do others see you?
  - How professional is your image?
  - How consistent are you with your appearance?
- What training would make you more easily pro-moted?
  - How well do you communicate? Ask others if you expect them to be mind readers, or if you fail to explain yourself fully.
  - How comfortable are you with sales? Sales are a part of business building. You are constantly selling yourself, your ideas, your proposals,

and your company. It's time to get comfortable with selling and asking for the close.

- How neat and organized is your published work? Your published work ranges from emails to letters to proposals to sales copy and anything else you write. If you have poor grammar, there are grammar apps you can use to help correct your writing.

- How proficient are you with the basic software packages that your business uses? Do you know Excel spreadsheets, QuickBooks, or whatever your company owns?

- How well do you know your company? When was the last time you reviewed your company policies and procedures? What about the company mission and vision?

- Finally, if you were your client, would you hire and promote your company?

Instead of choosing to be angry and eventually becoming bitter, you can refocus your brain on ways you can grow your business. By performing this simple exercise, your brain has already started to access your inner cowgirl, and I'll bet you have a list of many more questions you're asking yourself, with answers that are flooding your brain. When you evaluate your answers, you are now choosing to move in a positive direction, increase your strengths, and overcome your weaknesses.

If you're stuck and still feeling rejected, then perhaps your inner brat is whining and trying to be in control so that you don't get hurt again by getting your hopes up and then being told no. This is actually a form of self-sabotage. Thank your inner brat and let him or her know that you'll handle it from here.

Have you noticed that approaching your client and having a conversation with your client was not even in the personal inventory? Well you're right because now is not the time to question your clients. Your feelings might be a bit raw and it might be unwise to tempt yourself into choosing a negative syndrome. Now is the time to work on your inner inventory, increasing your awareness, and choosing the positive syndrome attitudes each day, each hour, and within each challenge.

At some time in the future when you're feeling secure and confident with yourself, it would be wise to call a meeting with your clients who did not buy and ask for feedback about your products, services, and your attitude. At that time, be prepared to hear things that you might not want to hear. Be grateful that they are telling you so that you can correct the issues. Also, ask what it would take to get the sale. Don't ask why they haven't hired or promoted you. That comes across as a bit of an attack, and they could easily become defensive and dismiss the conversation. Asking what it takes to get the sale and get promoted is forward focused, and it opens the discussion. Be prepared to listen without interrupting until they are done speaking. Allow the silence to sit in the air for at least 10 seconds. It might feel like an eternity. Then simply ask "what else?" Make certain that you give them time to ponder, gather their words, and answer. A good prospect will take his or her time to explain if you are gracious and secure enough to listen.

Wild Bull Chase

I have a punchy story about a time my friend John and I were rounding up a bull in a canyon pasture. I can hardly call it a pasture because there was only one small open area to graze. The rest of the ground was either rocky or filled with deep, thick brush and small trees. There was an old empty metal silo on one end of the canyon. An old barbed wire fence split the canyon in half, and the big, wild bull was on the far end of the canyon. A gravel road ran the length of the canyon, elevated a bit from the canyon floor. John was riding my favorite horse, a big black thoroughbred named Diesel. It was given to John because the horse was so mean, and nobody else could handle him. He was fast as lightning and strong too. I rode a small paint horse that was well behaved. We drove down the road with the truck and trailer, horses loaded and saddled, ready to run should we see the black bull. Towards the far end, we pulled over and parked the rig, unloaded, and decided to flush out that old bull. The dogs ran around sniffing as we rode through deep brush that was well over my knees at times, grabbing me from both sides.

All at once the dogs went to barking and the old, black bull started to scramble from his hiding place. John took off on Diesel with me following behind. I had a difficult time keeping up because Diesel was so fast and my little paint couldn't navigate the brush as well. I figured if I wanted to stay in the game, then I needed a new plan right then. I headed up to the road and off we went. From my new perspective, I could see brush moving and John following behind. I caught up to John and the bull, staying up on the road. At one point, the bull got tired and turned on John and Diesel. All I could see was Diesel coming up off the ground as that old, mean bull charged into him. John hung on, and they somehow got away. The bull headed off. John was so deep in brush he couldn't see the bull, so I became the spotter. We hollered back and forth, navigating the brush and creek until we came to the barbed wire fence. That old bull tried to jump the fence but fell tail over head in a complete somersault. John jumped up onto the road, around the fence and back down into the brush.

This bull was determined to lose us. When he spotted the old silo, he ran right inside and hid. John couldn't see where the bull went, so he hollered up to me, and I told him to look in the silo. He didn't believe me and even told me there was no way the bull would go in there. I assured him that the bull was in there hiding. John jumped off Diesel and snuck up to the silo as I watched from the road. Sure enough, old blackie was standing there in the dark, breathing heavily and hiding. We had to act quickly if we were going to capture him. I turned and raced down that road through the canyon back to the truck and trailer. I loaded up little paint and drove down to where the silo was. John backed the trailer up as close to the silo as possible. We had some gates, so we made a chute from the silo door to the trailer.

Now, to get the bull to come out was another trick. That darned bull was not coming out. I banged on the silo to scare him out but he still hid. We found a small hole in the wall, so I stuck a stick through it and tried to poke that bull so he'd run out the door. He was stubborn. After about 20 minutes of poking him and banging on the walls, John climbed up the short silo, pried part of the roof off and scared him out. Luckily, he ran down the makeshift chute and right into the trailer. John slammed the door shut. We loaded our horses behind the bull and let out a massive laugh. Mission accomplished.

Not once did we consider that we wouldn't find old blackie or that we wouldn't catch him. We weren't remembering the time we missed catching a wild cow. We weren't thinking about the fact that if anything happened, there were only two of us there in a canyon with no cell service. You might think that we were being irresponsible. We saw that there was a job to be done, and we assumed we would be successful. We were focused on one thing: capturing that mean old, black bull. We didn't get lost in the what-ifs. I could have felt sorry for myself that little paint couldn't keep up with Diesel; but instead, I positioned myself above the action, so I could help John navigate and I could stay in the game. Neither one of us took the glory; we shared that. That day in the canyon, my inner cowgirl took over and allowed me to experience a passionate, wild, exciting bull capture. Let your inner cowgirl meet you in your business arena so you too can experience passion and confidence as you successfully navigate your wild rides and mean bulls.

The bull chase isn't much different than building your business. John had a problem in that he needed to round up that wild black bull because he needed him to breed some cows in another pasture. I was able to help him solve his problem by being the spotter and retrieving the truck and trailer. I accompanied him with a servant's heart. That's the most effective way to build a sustainable business, through a servant's heart. When people know you truly care about helping them solve their problems, then they trust you quicker. They feel that you're not after their money but that you truly care about them.

Part of letting your inner cowgirl shine is letting people know you love what you do and that you care about them. You aren't doing what you do just for the money. You truly want to make their life easier and better. They will quickly like and trust you and promote you to other prospective clients.

COWGIRL GRIT:
SCRAP THE PAST TO LAUNCH FAST

If it doesn't seem to be worth the effort, it probably isn't.

Cowgirl Grit. It's what's at the heart of every cowgirl. It makes her who and what she is. So what is grit? It's the pulsing vein that runs deep inside that keeps you going when you want to quit. It's the small voice whispering to try one more time. It whispers to try something just a little differently until you find the way, the answer, or the solution. Just. Keep. Trying.

When our horse has grit, we also call it "try." It's when the horse doesn't quit on you. When you're roping and your horse shoots out of the box chasing the steer, he doesn't quit halfway down the arena. He keeps going until you rope those horns and turn him, or until you reach the end of the arena. His heart is in the performance full force, and he doesn't stop until you stop him. Each time you ask, he tries. That is try, or grit. It's the focus and the toughness of mind, body, and spirit.

Grit

Grit is comprised of three components: strength, bravery, and drive. Whether you're riding in the rodeo arena or showing up to a sales call, grit is needed to make your presence known. One thing about grit that is very important to understand is that it does not have anger as its foundation. In fact, anger is not any part of grit. You don't need anger to have grit. I've known some people who use anger to exert their power and show their grit. This is not true power or grit. It's simply using fear to provide a false image of power and grit.

The person who has grit is kind, gentle, compassionate, and fun. They are that way because they are secure in who they are. They don't need to prove anything to anyone. They simply love what they do and give it 150% of their awareness and energy. Anger, on the other hand, is a lower form of energetic relationship that uses fear and manipulation and eventually becomes ineffective. A person who chooses anger usually feels threatened in some way because they perceive the situation from a negative, fearful perspective.

The strengths needed for grit are mental, emotional, and physical. Mental strength is the ability to focus on a project until the solution is found and the project is completed. It means that the job is finished and distractions are ignored.

The emotionally strong person does not whine or continue to replay unresolved issues. They resolve the issue in an unemotional way. How do you do that? You let go of controlling the outcome and become curious about the situation. Ask questions. Be a researcher. Find the root cause of the problem. Sometimes simply exposing the root cause will help the problem to dissipate. Either way, being curious and exposing the root cause gives a foundation from which to start formulating a solution. The emotionally strong person responds rather than reacting. They take a few moments to consider the facts, ask what might be underlying the facts, and then proceed with curiosity.

A person who is mentally and emotionally strong will tend to have more physical energy because they aren't using their energy on negative thoughts or replaying negative scenarios and harmful conversations. Think about someone you know who is depressed. They sit around and have no energy because their mind and emotions have sucked the physical life out of them. So, having true grit is a physically energetic way of going.

Bravery

Bravery is the piece that spurs a cowgirl into action. Without bravery, it's very difficult to move forward, jump into action, ask for the promotion, and build your business. Bravery, or courage, does not mean that you're not afraid. It means that you take that fear, say hello, and take action anyway.

When I was riding the welted horse and bucking on the side of the butte, I was afraid. And, I'm not afraid to admit that I was afraid. That could have quickly become ugly, and I could have gotten bucked off, kicked, stepped on, and ended up with broken bones, having to be airlifted out of there. Instead I made the choice to ride through those bucks and exert my power, without getting mad. I was just matter of fact. Hello, fear! This could get ugly, but for now, I'm going to be brave, find my grit, and ride through this situation.

You too are a brave person. Look at all that you have already dealt with. You've tolerated situations and jobs. You've tried other ventures, failed, and tried again. That takes courage. You could have quit and walked away. And in fact, you might make the conscious decision that this is simply not the time to build a business, but you need to be certain that you're making a conscious choice to not take action. You need to be certain that you're making the choice to stay put rather than build a business and promote yourself. However, staying put and not taking action when the real reason is that you are too afraid to push through is not cowgirl grit. It's not bravery or courage. So, consider deep down if you're being hobbled by fear, or motivated by conscious bravery. It's a tricky thin, gray line, but deep in your gut or your heart, you know the answer.

Drive

Drive is the part of grit that keeps you going. It is the motivating force that makes you get back into the saddle and ride again even after you've been bucked off or failed at other business ventures. Drive is an admirable trait to have and something that people will look for in someone to do business with.

Now do not confuse drive with overworking. Overworking is simply doing a bunch of busy work that could be outsourced to a virtual assistant. Overworking might be tweaking a website for the tenth time or rewriting an email for the eighth time which takes time away from your productivity, ultimately costing you precious time away from your horses.

Drive is the energy behind the focus that moves a project or sale towards completion. Drive is about getting it done within the timeframe you have set, rather than letting it linger with no deadline. The person with drive shows up ready to go instead of playing at the coffee machine or scrolling through social media for 45 minutes before getting down to business.

Past Stories

A very important point about grit is that you can't be holding onto your past and have grit. If you're constantly mulling over what happened yesterday, or the day before, or last quarter, then you're focusing on the unresolved issues in your past and cannot possibly be focused on the present. I suggest perhaps writing a list of all the things that you continually whine about. If you can't come up with that list, ask someone with whom you spend free time. They will certainly be able to help you make your list because they will know the stories that you keep telling over and over without resolution. Call your best friend and ask her to be totally honest and raw with you. You have to listen and not react because most likely you won't like what you hear. Thank her for being brave and sharing. This is a wonderful gift she is giving you.

When you have your list, then either write a letter to anyone appearing in any of the scenarios, forgiving them for whatever you feel they have done that has hurt you. If you want, you can send the letter to them, but not until it's rested in your possession for at least a week, and you've read it at least once every day. If you still feel the need to send it, then do it. Many times, just the act of writing the letter and forgiving that person is enough to process the situation. Releasing the anger, betrayal, or whatever emotion you are feeling will be cathartic. Also, thank them for the lessons they have taught you. In fact, consider that through the process of confronting them and forgiving them, you are learning to process your emotions, respond instead of react, and reframe the whole situation.

Reframing the situation gives you a new, fresh perspective of what happened. Consider the situation from the other person's standpoint. Maybe communication was poor and assumptions were made. Those assumptions may have grown into rifts, and nobody was brave enough to cross the chasm until now. Congratulate yourself if you have done this exercise. The more you look at situations from multiple perspectives, the easier it is to respond unemotionally because you're not jumping to your default reaction.

Reframing a situation also helps you to uncover a win-win-win solution. That's a solution where both sides and the team wins. It's a solution that neither side started with, but one that grew out of you being able to reframe the problem and see it from a higher perspective. The more you practice this skill, the easier and more natural it becomes. This type of skill is one that gets a person promoted and the business built because you are the rainmaker, the problem solver, and the 8-second rider. You get it done when nobody else can.

Sometimes we need to examine our past failures so that we can learn from them and avoid repeating them. This is not a new concept. A cowgirl will most certainly remember the time she left the pasture gate open, and the bull went into the neighbor's pasture and frolicked with his cows. She'll think twice next time she goes through a gate. She'll double-check it, maybe even triple-check it.

The same goes for business building, promoting yourself, and making sales. So, you made 100 sales calls and didn't get a sale. Take a good, close look and be honest with yourself. Would you have bought what you offered? If you were your friend, would you have bought from your friend and promoted her to others? If you're being honest, you should be able to see some behaviors that could either be changed or strengthened. This is not easy work. It's also not meant to make you feel like a failure. In fact, if you feel like a failure then you're not focusing on the solution. Don't jump into being emotional or whiny.

Here's an example of how to process a past failure. Way back in high school, I was in the advanced writing class my senior year. The final paper was an autobiography. I had struggled through the class because for some reason, no matter how much effort I put into a paper, it was never good enough. So, I was determined to get an A on this final paper. How difficult could an autobiography be to write? I wrote my paper, rewrote it, edited it, and re-edited it. I was certain it was an amazing paper. After all, I knew and liked the subject! When the graded paper was returned, there was only a red comment on the top to see the teacher. I stayed after class to talk to her, and she accused me of plagiarism! Plagiarism? It was my life story for darn sake! The teacher ended up giving me an A after I argued that it couldn't possibly have been copied because it was completely about me, and she was free to call my parents for verification. The scar she left on me, led me to make future choices based on her accusation. When I went to college, I chose a major that did not include any writing, only multiple choice or short answer tests. In my corporate jobs and businesses, I never offered to write up sales copy or proposals. My reports always followed a template. I lived in fear that I would be called a fraud. That certainly wasn't my inner cowgirl shining through.

Acknowledging the fear of writing, putting it away, and finding my inner cowgirl meant identifying the driving force behind my choices and letting go of that teacher's opinion. It's funny that I can't even remember her name anymore. It takes a conscious choice followed by forward action to say goodbye to fear, find your grit, and step out with bravery. I since have spent years writing a company newsletter and have over 90 editions written. I am a writer and published author now because I've let my inner cowgirl shine through. You can do this too by finding those underlying driving forces and acknowledging them, which rids them of their power. Then, say hello to bravery. Remember, bravery is doing something in spite of your fear. It's time to find that inner cowgirl and let her take the lead. She's the strong, intelligent, brave, driven, fun leader that's inside you. Let her out for Pete's sake, so we can get to building your business!

9

FROM COWBOSS TO CEO

Nobody ever drowned himself in his own sweat.

We have spent quite some time laying the foundation for starting a business. What we also need to address is who you will be in your new business as you promote yourself. Smart business building includes a strong foundation. I'm going to challenge you to consider what you truly want so that you can create your forward path in a way that honors your values and goals.

The Cowgirl Code you created in Chapter 4 will come in handy as we discuss your next steps. This may seem trivial and you might want to skim over this chapter or skip it completely, but this is paramount for creating the business you want that will light up your spirit, keep you motivated and happy, and give you more time with your horses. So grab your code and let's ride!

A cowboss is the hired hand that runs the cattle operation on the ranch. He usually answers to a general manager but might answer to the owner if there is no general manager. The cowboss hires and fires the cowboys because he spends the most time with them. He chooses where the cowboys will ride in relation to the herd. He designates who rides point, or in front of the herd, leading the herd and giving the herd something to follow. He designates the flank riders, the cowboys who ride alongside the herd, keeping it together. He designates the drag rider, the cowboy riding behind the herd, pushing the stragglers and slow cattle to keep up with the herd. He manages the jigger boss, the cowboy who makes sure the horses are fed and cared for. The jigger also ropes the cowboys' horses and brings them into the corral so they can be saddled up.

You might be the drag rider, feeling left out and left behind quite often. You might feel like you are working on an island with very little conversation and personal interaction. The drag rider is possibly one of the most important people. While cattle need someone to follow, they are moved into action from the pushing force behind. This, however, might not be the spot for you if you value relationships. Being the drag rider is good for the introvert. Sure, he must communicate, but he's totally happy with his thoughts. In your current job, you might think that point rider is a promotion because you see that person in front of you all the time, but really, it's a lateral move. Both of you report to the cowboss. Understanding where you are in your current job and how you interact with your team will help you decide if you want to stay or if you want to transition into a business owner position. Let's create your CEO position that better fits and honors your values and goals.

Right now, take out a piece of paper, or your journal, and write down your ideal CEO job description. What do you want to do? What are your responsibilities? What would showcase your skills? Where do you feel like work is effortless and fun? How many days per week do you want to work? Do you want to spend some time in the office and some time traveling? Do you enjoy doing presentations or meeting one-on-one with clients? Do you love or hate sales? Create whatever ideal job description you can that would compel you to move across the country in order to do it. It needs to be something so sweet you can hardly contain your excitement.

Look at some job listings on the major sites online for template ideas. You will see that most do not post salary because that truly should not be the motivating factor.

Companies know that if they hire someone who is motivated by money, that person will quickly fizzle out and leave. They ultimately won't be happy unless they are continually receiving raises or bonuses. The key piece is that you love what you do. The money will follow. You will set money goals later. For now, write your ideal job.

On a side note, many times people who feel crunched for more money simply are not living within their means. They are trying to keep up with the neighbors or impress someone or fill a void in their spirit. If that's you, then I suggest you investigate why money is the most important goal for you. What are you proving by overspending? What feeling do you get from spending money, and how can you get that feeling from something else that is more positive?

Within your own ideal job description, it's important to list with bullet points everything for which you will be held accountable. Your responsibilities should also be the items for which you are accountable. Describe your level of authority. Who do you oversee? Who reports to you? Since you're just starting, you probably don't have any employees, but it's important to consider whom you will hire to help you once you get going. Maybe you'll outsource your sales calls, or your social media management, or your accounting and taxes. Include this information also: To whom do you report and how often? You will want either a coach or an accountability partner. Yes, this is a detailed description. Outlining these boundaries will save you from wandering into terrain that isn't your ideal trail.

Let's discuss the experience piece of the description. Be sure to list what kinds of experience would be important to your ideal job. Do not get tripped up on whether you currently have that experience or not. The point here is to create your ideal job description. If you are lacking some of the experience needed for your ideal description, then you've written your description just fine. That's perfect. This is the opportunity for you to identify what additional training you need. It's also important because you'll know what past experiences you have that don't need to be showcased. Many times, people list all kinds of things they have done on their resume, hoping that the hiring manager will be impressed. Don't waste time with fluff.

Another side point is that you need to keep a working resume at all times that you update as you grow. The reason this step is important is that when you start marketing and promoting yourself and your business, you can use some of this information from your ideal CEO description in your marketing. You will want to tell the world what your ideal dream business is so that you aren't expected to do something else, and you don't give in to doing things that aren't in alignment with your goals, values, and dream business.

Most importantly, I want you to be certain of where you're heading and that your new business will serve you well. You need to fit into your CEO position as if it's your favorite pair of boots, so comfortable you could sleep in them.

Let's go back to your experience. You've created your list of experiences. How close does that align with your ideal business? What areas do you need further training and education? Make a list of those things. They might include communication, leadership, team building, software, proposal writing, technical skills, image coaching, or anything else that comes to mind.

Look at your competition and see if you can identify traits that they have that maybe you could improve. Make friends with your competition. They could become your partner and certainly could be your source of referrals or someone you can refer to if you don't want to or can't serve a potential client. This is another small step to getting in the game. You'll also learn what their challenges are and where their gaps lie. This is very helpful for you as you build your business. Find out where they're struggling. You might also struggle there, and you can partner up to solve that problem for yourselves and others. If you don't struggle where they are struggling, then you can help them overcome their challenges and they become a client as an additional stream of income.

There are a lot of places to secure training for business building, in general, as well as in the equine industry. If you choose to sell someone else's product, then they should provide free training. If you're creating your own product, then you won't need training on your product, but you might need training in other areas such as computer spreadsheets, videography, or email marketing. If you want to learn banding and braiding, simply ask someone to teach you. Sometimes they will teach you for free and sometimes they might charge a small fee. You can also find gobs of equine how-to videos on YouTube. Community colleges provide training in photography, graphic design, and accounting. You can even ask your competition where they obtained their training. Sometimes it's listed on their website.

Identify what you need to learn for your skill or product by looking at your job description and seeing where your knowledge gaps lie. Don't get hung up on the fact that you don't have the training and experience. Giving the nod to open the bucking chute gate opens your world to obtaining the knowledge and experience you will use. As a new business, people don't expect expert-level products and services. Just be honest. There are people who will hire you based on your honesty, integrity, and guarantee.

Look at any of your professional organizations. They usually hold training events at their annual conventions.

Also, there are thousands of online training courses, but this will take some research since the training can range from cheap to expensive. Don't just look at reviews. Ask on forums. Post questions on Facebook sites. Look on LinkedIn. I've taken some great training programs from sites you would not imagine. One single mom became an expert at WordPress and offered a really great online video training. I think I paid $97 and now know how to create and manage a website using WordPress. There are other sites that host trainings for anybody who can create a program. I'd buy a cheap course from an author first to see how I liked their course before jumping into their prime offers. Some of them will give you a free course lesson. There are also a ton of free training programs if you sign up for the email list. Harvard Law School's program on negotiation has a newsletter with a lot of good information. They publish a variety of free reports. It's best to consider a program that has a certificate of completion or certification because they can give you credibility.

Money

I am going to switch gears and talk about the money part of promotion. If you're moving from drag rider to point rider, you might expect a raise because you're leading the herd. In reality, you're still part of the team driving the herd, so no raise. If you move from point rider to cowboss, you might also expect a raise, and you might get one. You're still someone's employee, so your salary is a fixed income. Sometimes your compensation comes in the form of money and sometimes it comes in the form of benefits or perks. Maybe you get to pick your tent site first when you reach camp. It's important to consider what your goals are and what is acceptable compensation for you. If it's all about the money, as I said before, then you really need to reconsider why money is your motivating factor, and how to better live within your means.

There's a funny thing about the universe. When you talk about always needing money, you're telling the universe that you are in need. If you live within your means and spend less than you earn, then you will naturally feel abundance. In order to grow that abundance, you must be thankful and grateful. Thank those who support you and give you anything, whether money, objects, or intangibles, such as referrals. Act gratefully by giving back to those people and by paying it forward to someone else. This could be through giving a gift, doing a favor, or being a support system for someone.

When I was very sick and almost didn't make it to my next birthday, I had some friends step forward and bring me food. They checked in on me regularly, sometimes daily. They might, hopefully, never be in the same situation where I can cook food and help them regain their health. I can, however, find someone else who needs help and be available to him or her. Of course, thanking my friends who made the food and continually checked in on me is absolutely required.

The point is that if your main goal is chasing money, then money will put up a good chase and elude you often. Money is simply a form of energy. We exchange time for money, or ideas, or intelligence, or whatever. It's simply an exchange. Therefore, you can't chase it and try to capture it without some exchange. It's actually easier to attract money by giving first. Be brave and let go of the need for money so that the money finds you passionately doing what you love.

Regarding money, I also strongly believe in giving to others. I support my church and a couple of other non-profit groups that I have vetted well. Be sure that if you're donating money that the group doesn't pay their CEO a huge chunk of money, but that the money truly goes to provide for those less fortunate. Pick your favorite charity that is in alignment with those values that you created and give a specific amount each month.

Tools

Ropes, spurs, a good horse, and a great cattle dog are the tools a cowgirl needs. Identifying the tools you will need in your new business is a way to prepare for the transition from job to business. Identifying your resources is the best place to start. Find the professional organizations and look into the resources they provide that might apply to your business. You might not know the exact tools you'll need so knowing where to go to find them when you do need them will help you to perform efficiently.

Some of you may be wondering when we will talk about the nuts and bolts of the business. Even though we aren't there yet, I'll write a short bit that you can tuck into your saddlebag. Set yourself up as a sole proprietorship if it's just you and no employees. You can change to a limited liability corporation, C-corp or S-corp later. You don't need to start with a website, but if you are proficient and want to spend the money, then go for it. Either way, I'd buy the URL for your company name through namecheap or godaddy. Set up a Facebook page, Instagram page, and Pinterest page for your product or service. Obtain your business license from your local government. The business license process may take several weeks because most applications require public announcements such as published newspaper ads. Your local government can guide you on obtaining your license. Set up an email autoresponder account so you can start building an email list of clients and prospective clients. You don't need a big fancy website or online store unless that's what your business will be. It's more important to start testing your product or service than to invest in a bunch of backup business items. That will grow over time.

One of the final points to orchestrating your transition from cowboss to CEO involves your private life. It is unhealthy for your whole life to revolve around your job, even if you love what you're doing. Everyone needs to rest from work, or they'll burn out. So, look again at your goals to be sure that you have a balance between your goals, your work, and your personal life. What do you do in your free time? What makes you laugh? How much rest do you need to function well? Who do you love to spend time with? You absolutely need to ensure that you have free time that involves laughter, fun and the people you value. This will keep your mind functioning in a creative, positive mode, which is the basis for your business. Even though your business is allowing you to live your passion, you still need to take a break, enjoy a vacation, and spend time with your loved ones who might share other passions.

CREATE YOUR POSSE:
BUILD YOUR FOLLOWING

If you're ridin' ahead of the herd, take a look back every now and then to make sure it's still there with ya.

A key component to building your business and getting promoted is identifying your followers. We discussed that in Chapter 5 when we looked at who was in your arena. We are going to dive deeper into team creation and follower identification. You need to have your people who support and help you, and to whom you also serve, along on your journey. Choosing these people wisely will serve you well as a foundation for building your business. While it's easy to choose friends, they might not always be able to look at you and your journey objectively.

A cowgirl will have her people, or, as I call them, her posse, who work with her on a regular basis. She might have a riding coach who watches her and gives her feedback. She might also have an accountant who takes care of her finances. She could also have her buckaroos, the cowboys who take care of her livestock. These are all necessary people. When it comes time to brand all the calves, not all of those people will be helping. The accountant isn't going to grab a vaccine gun or branding iron or hold a calf down for the brander. Thus, the cowgirl will probably call on others to come help. These people who show up to help and ask nothing in return are also part of her posse. They support her because they care about her. Her buckaroos will be helping because they work for her and probably care about her too. If nothing else, they care about their job and want the herd to be fully branded for the wellbeing of the business and their job. Her posse is made up of the people that show up when there's work to be done. They want her to succeed.

Who is your posse? Who are the people that show up when you need help? Who is your reliable go-to person for help? Depending on your business, this may be a partner. Maybe there's a mentor who has taken an interest in helping groom you for promotion and business building. It's important to identify at least five people who you can call your posse. They don't need to be involved directly in your business, or even the equine industry, but having at least one or two that are intimately familiar with horses will be helpful. They can provide insight that outsiders won't have. Choose people who have already achieved success in one or more areas of their lives. Choose those who are willing to support and guide you and will be available. Choose those who aren't dealing with current struggles in their own lives. If you are able, choose people who are gifted in different areas. Maybe one person is a successful trainer, another possesses financial savvy, and another knows horse showing and is a judge or organizes shows. Finally, another might have great wisdom with life circumstances, knowing how to deal effectively with conflict resolution.

It is not a great idea to choose family or friends for your posse because they could be too close emotionally. They might not see you how your colleagues and clients see you. They might not be encouraging because they don't really want to see you succeed. It would make them feel less successful. Or, they think that you're the greatest person in the universe who can do no wrong, next to Jesus Christ. Either way, most of the time friends and family come to the table with baggage or preconceived ideas that will not serve you in building your business.

Since this is a team that you have composed of handpicked people, not one assigned to you, the team building might look a little different. Your team at work consists of people that you either work with, work for, or who work for you. Your posse consists of people that will primarily work with you, some of them being from the horse industry. The work isn't circled around work tasks but around building and growing your business. It is more visionary. Your posse will need to be nurtured and cared for in more personal ways than your work team. It's important to be able to separate your work team from your posse because there might be some small overlaps.

Your posse needs to know you a little more personally than your work team. For example, you might share that you went on a date with your significant other last weekend and saw a current movie. You wouldn't elaborate on the fact that your significant other made you feel terrible because he complained through the movie about how stupid it was and then proceeded to stare at other women during dinner. You might, however, mention that to your posse so that they can help you process the experience and create a plan for how to deal with it should it happen again. This is a prime example of why your friends and family wouldn't be good posse members. I don't know about you, but my close friends and family would be showing up at my significant other's doorstep fully engaged in Gunslinger Syndrome if they thought he hurt me.

Sharing life struggles with your posse helps them know you better, guide and advise you better, and hold you accountable for making positive changes. They can help you with personal challenges because personal challenges are usually similar to professional challenges, just two different arenas. Of course, you want them to help guide you with any professional challenges too.

Nurturing your posse means staying in contact with them on a regular basis. That might mean a simple phone call to check in or meeting for a cup of coffee. Perhaps you take them out for dinner once a month or to a sporting event. You should always remember their birthdays and send physical cards. That happens so infrequently but is such an easy action to take. Do it if you want to stand out from the crowd. It's not lame; it's smart to make people feel remembered. Send a card just because it's funny, or send an email telling them that you appreciate all that they have done for you. Too often people are not thanked nor made to feel appreciated. If you know they like a certain candy or coffee, buy them a box of candy or bag of coffee and gift it to them next time you see them. Nurturing your posse takes some creativity but mostly action. Nurturing will mold them into your most loyal fans and help you stand out like a punchy cowgirl walking through Times Square.

Listening

The most important action you can take with your posse is listening. When you ask for help, support, advice, or feedback, you need to listen. So, let's talk about this for a minute. Listening is super important because that's how you learn. Most people think they are listening when they sit quietly for a few seconds, but I'd bet they aren't listening at all, or maybe just 10-15% listening. Most people hear one sentence or maybe only the first few words that the other person has spoken before they jump into formulating the next thing they want to say. Many times, the habitual interrupters are these people. They don't listen worth a darn, and they're so bent on letting everyone else know how much they know that they interrupt and talk right over you. They need assurance, acknowledgment, and validation that they indeed are smart and have good ideas. The problem is that some of these people are an empty well that can't be filled no matter how much acknowledgement you give.

Sometimes, however, you might need to interrupt in order to take control of a conversation that is running away down a negative path or simply to see if the person to whom you are speaking has any idea that they are interrupting and talking over you. Many times, the interrupters don't even know they're doing it.

When a cowgirl is riding, whether it's in the arena, or on the open range, she is listening. In fact, she has a heightened sense about her. Certainly, her horse is not going to start talking in English. Mr. Ed is the only one who does that! She is listening for the slither of a snake or the gurgle of a creek or the breaking of branches on the ground. She wants to hear the small noises that most people wouldn't notice because that's where she can figure out where the water runs, or who or what might be sneaking up on her, or where the snake den lies. When you're conversing with anyone, but especially your posse, listen to their words, and also listen to what is in between their words. Listen to their tone of voice, intonation, loudness or softness, and the silences. Learn to be comfortable in the silence because you will learn much in the silence.

When I'm closing a client on a several thousand-dollar proposal, I sit in silence as soon as I disclose the price. I don't go into justifying it or offering to discount it. I sit in silence. I wait until they say something. I give them time to process the cost. I also watch their body language and facial expression. Then, I prepare for whatever response they give me. If I've done a great job selling the proposal up front, then they usually say they're ready to get started. Sometimes they comment on how costly the proposal is. I acknowledge and validate them saying, "yes, it's costly, but it's more costly for you to stay where you're at and live with the problems you've been living with." Sometimes they give an objection or excuse about how it's not going to work. Right then, I know they probably aren't someone I want to work with, but I'll at least be curious and ask what part they believe won't work. If I hear more empty excuses, I usually tell them that I don't think they want the results badly enough, and I don't want them to spend a bunch of money and be unsuccessful. They either walk out and I'm done wasting my time, or they decide to do it. Sometimes they have a valid reason that the plan isn't feasible for them and we can quickly change it so they can get started.

You should know that most of that process involved me observing them and listening to their silence. I can hear the crickets across the road sometimes. Remember, listening is learning. It's not formulating your next response. It's paying attention to the small things happening in the other person. Good listening also puts you in control because you learn what motivates the other person or what advice they can share or what bad experiences they've had and how you can avoid them. Simply put, you won't learn from hearing yourself talk. Listening is also a form of respect. So, when you're listening to one of your posse members, you're making them feel valued and respected. Sometimes that's the greatest gift a person can give to another.

Branding

Once your posse is formed and they have agreed to mentor or support you, then we also need to look at who you want to be. Creating a personal brand is a great way to stand out. Consider Scott Shellady, the CowGuy. He's well known in the stocks and commodities fields and is on television regularly. Now, I doubt Scott rides horses or owns cows. However, he sure does know how to brand himself. Watch him on television and see how he wears the same Holstein cow pattern jacket with a bow tie every time he's interviewed. It's great branding because everyone remembers the jacket and thus Scott. Scott has made himself stand out and has become the go-to guy for commodities. What do you want to be the go-to cowgirl for? What do you want people to think of you for when they need that thing?

The first step in branding is figuring out your micro-niche. If you're a logo creator, your micro-niche could be hunt seat riders, or Quarter Horse stallions, or Arabian farms. If you're a website creator, you could build and maintain websites for Paint Horse breeding operations. That one thing is whatever you love to do. In your professional arena, what one thing do you want to be the one to whom everyone considers the expert? Once you know your micro-niche, you can add needed skills to your training list.

Don't be afraid to pick a micro-niche. It doesn't mean that you won't get other people wanting you to serve them too. It just means that you have a specific product or service that you market to a specific group of people. As I mentioned earlier, your business will morph as you grow.

Branding yourself so that you stand out means letting that inner cowgirl out. Scott Shellady could have been afraid of what people would say about his cow jacket, but he wasn't. He let his inner cowboy lead the way with courage and intuition. Your personal brand can also be a clothing item. Maybe you love wild rags, the large silk scarves that cowgirls wear. Or maybe you love wearing cowboy boots because your feet are always cold. Wear them! Be sure that the rest of your attire is professional and clean. You can wear nice, clean, black cowboy boots with dress slacks and that could be part of your brand. You might love the color purple, so you wear some purple item every single day. That could be part of your brand.

Your brand can also include a behavior. Maybe you yodel for every sale closed over $10K. Maybe you bring a favorite brand of pretzels to work every Thursday. Maybe you do a five second happy dance at 3PM every day when the staff is feeling the after lunch sluggish hour. Be creative! However you brand yourself, you want to be certain that it is in alignment with your business policies, mission statement, values and morals. I would recommend not having any part of your brand relating to politics. That's a murky ocean that can cause a stampede in no time. Steer clear of anything political, unless, of course, your business is somehow politically related to horses.

Action Plans

One of the ways to successfully manage your posse is through an action plan. Some people call it goal setting. Goals are very important, as we've previously discussed. An action plan is more detailed and time oriented. The action plans are not for the posse but for you. You will create your personal and professional action plans and then share them with your posse. Let your posse know that these are the things that you want to accomplish within the stated time frames and that you need their help. If you have chosen the right posse then they will be jumping to get started. If they aren't excited, then you need to go back to step one and reconsider who should be part of your posse.

I love using spreadsheets to create action plans because I can easily add or delete steps. I can highlight in color code when something is completed, or when I am waiting on help or resources. Your personal action plan should consist of things such as horses, relationships, living arrangements, hobbies, children, family, car maintenance, license plates, or anything else pertaining to your personal life. Your professional action plan will include business building, marketing and promotions, training, work projects, business relationships, personal branding, professional organization memberships, and anything else related to business growth. I list each item in a column on the left. Under each item, I list the steps needed to accomplish the task. I am very specific with including all steps. All the rest of the columns are dates. I like to use dates that fall on Mondays to identify the week. I simply put an X in the column for which I want to accomplish the action step. Once it's accomplished, I highlight it in purple, my celebration color. You can use any color you like and that makes you feel good. If I have a deadline approaching for a task and I know I'll need help, I highlight it yellow. Red is for items that I've missed. I highlight red then add another X in a column further out to readjust the date. I also look to see if I need to add an action step and that's the reason I didn't complete that step or if there was another reason. It's easy to add a row and type in a forgotten action step.

You will probably spend several days to a week, in divided increments, creating your action plans. This is another task that I see a lot of women skip over, thinking that it's just busy work. Yes, it takes time, but you will earn back far more time from organizing your goals, breaking them down into steps, and giving yourself a due date. Dreams can only be achieved when plans are put into action.

Share your action plans with your posse and be open to feedback. They might play devil's advocate, or they might point out where some action steps might be better arranged, or both. Perhaps they will identify where you omitted some steps. This is where their collective wisdom will help guide you to success. This is your springboard for standing out as a business owner in the equine arena. When you take the entire context that you learned in prior chapters and infuse it into a detailed action plan, then success will come with each action step.

Cowgirls get things done with style and spirit. That's what's so attractive about cowgirls. They spring into action with courage. Don't let them fool you though. They are good, careful planners. They don't just show up in the arena on a horse they don't know and try to run barrels without having prepared and planned. They put hours and hours into planning and preparation so that when they show up, they show up to stand out and be successful. So, go meet your inner cowgirl for a cup of hot coffee and get to work creating your action plans. You'll be glad you did.

HERDING YOUR HUMANS: CONFLICT RESOLUTION

*You don't need decorated words to make your meanin'
clear.
Say it plain and save some breath for breathin'.*

No matter how hard you try to avoid it, conflict will find you. It's part of life, and part of relationships. Keeping your herd of humans around you in a peaceful manner takes savvy and skill. Dealing with conflict is inevitable unless you're an ostrich and enjoy living life with your head buried in the sand. So, let's talk about when to engage in conflict and how to best resolve conflict.

I have a simple barometer I use to help me determine when to engage in the conflict and when to simply let it pass right on by. Some people call it choosing your battles. If the conflict hurts a person, including me, then I address it. If the conflict violates my morals or values, then I address it. Otherwise, it's not usually worth my time, attention, or energy. Now that's a simplistic view, but it does work most of the time. Sometimes you are involved with another person who simply wants to fight. I sat in a meeting recently with someone who started the meeting by saying, "Don't push me. I'm ready for a fight." Of course, my initial thought was, "Wow. This could be fun to see how far I can push to start the fight." I didn't bother pushing…or responding. I simply let those words sit right there in air space until that person spoke again. I wondered if the other person heard the echo of those words. Nonetheless, the rest of the meeting went fine because I chose not to engage and draw my guns. In essence, I was the one controlling the tone of the meeting by my conscious choices rather than by emotionally reacting.

Choosing when to engage in the Gunslinger Syndrome and when to keep your guns holstered is a skill that all business owners must hone. Actually, the best way to dispel a conflict is not always approaching it with guns ablazin', but instead with curiosity. Managing conflict starts before the conflict elevates into harsh words and abrupt actions. It involves solving small, seemingly trivial problems, as well as large, roadblock problems.

One thing I want to address is the whole let's agree to disagree idea. To me, this is simply an acknowledgment that we are in a standoff. Nothing has been resolved. No solution has been created. We are simply saying, "yep, there's a big chasm, and we are not going to build a bridge to connect our sides." The funny thing about those chasms is that they tend to quietly grow, and eventually, it's difficult to see across the chasm. It's akin to sweeping the issue under the rug and expecting that you won't trip on the rug every time you stroll across it. So, let's commit to one of two things: either completely let go of the conflict or find a resolution.

Letting go of a conflict means that you allow the other person to control whatever the issue is. That means for instance if you want to eat at one restaurant, and they want to eat at another, you choose to let them pick and you don't harbor any negative feelings or harsh words now or ever. You don't bring it up again, and you don't secretly hold it against them, tallying the score. Letting go means you forget that the issue ever arose. Period. End of issue. There is a freedom in this method because you don't waste time or energy on something that isn't terribly important. After all, this is not your last meal so you'll likely be eating at both restaurants eventually. Two questions you can ask yourself to see if letting go is the right thing to do in a given situation are:

1. How important is this issue to you on a scale of 0 to10?
2. Why is it that important?

Answering these two questions will help put the conflict into perspective and also help you decide if it's worth your energy and attention. If you rate an issue at a 5 out of 10 for importance, but can't even justify why it's that important, then reconsider your rating, or continue to investigate an underlying reason for the rating.

Make the Right Thing Easy

Managing people is a lot like managing horses. You can't drag a horse around and expect him to follow willingly. The same is true for managing people. If you are bossy and controlling and try to force people into doing things, then they are going to pull back and resist. Now, if I'm working with a horse and I'm trying to train him to do a certain action, then I'll make it as easy as possible for him to succeed. Maybe I want him to walk through a gate. I'll point him to the gate, walk him towards the gate at a comfortable pace, and walk right on through not making a big deal of anything until he's done what I want. Then I praise him.

Let's say he walks up to the gate but then jumps back trying to drag me 15 feet backwards. Well, now I have to make it very uncomfortable for him, so I'll make him work harder. I'll lunge him in a small circle until he's tired and decides that he wants to do what I want him to do. There's no force or anger. I don't pet him and console him for being naughty. I don't make excuses that he's afraid. If he were afraid, he would stop and look but still respect me being on the end of that lead line. There's a difference between fear and rebellion. The key is to make it difficult to do the things you don't want, and make it easy to do the things you do want. That same principle applies to managing your people.

Managing conflict from the starting gate is a proactive way to deal with it. That means that you have clear communication and assume that the other person is not a mind reader. You speak clearly, listen often and well, and clarify any small misunderstanding so they don't become large misunderstandings. A lot of conflicts could be avoided if communication was clear, concise, and honest from the beginning. When people are afraid to communicate kindly or just don't want to, then the rift starts.

So, you want to build a following and get promoted? Make it difficult for your clients and prospective customers to *not* promote you by standing out as the servant leader and expert. Make it easy to promote you by being ready to help solve their challenges. When they consider hiring you and promoting you and they find out how ready you are to smoothly step up and help them solve their problems because you have prepared yourself, then they will also look like they've made a smart choice.

Some of your prospective customers might seem irritated and even try to create conflict. They are probably the ones that need you the most and don't even realize it. They have a problem and can't identify it, but they know deep down they are in pain or discomfort. They need something fixed in themselves or help overcoming a challenge but don't have a clue what that is, so they lash out at you and others trying to fix you, or mock you, or are just plain mean.

In this situation, it's important to set your boundaries by going back to your values and Cowgirl Code. What will you accept? How can you communicate nicely what is acceptable treatment and behavior towards you? When telling that person what you will accept you must be very clear and concrete. Remember, they don't realize they have a problem deep inside, so you have to first focus on the concrete behaviors before you can dive deeper into what's underneath and motivating their harsh actions and words.

When I was having phone conversations with one of my former husbands during our divorce, he would call and literally scream at me on the phone. I would tell him in a calm, lower tone of voice, speaking slowly, that if he did not speak to me nicely, then I would hang up. If he continued, then I gave him one more warning that I was hanging up, and then I hung up. He usually called right back, and we continued this game for a few more rounds. That only happened a few times, and he realized that I would no longer accept being treated like a doormat. When I respected myself and told him how to treat me, he learned quickly how to behave. We haven't had another argument in over 10 years. People will treat you how they want to treat you unless you nicely tell them otherwise.

If you're trying to motivate your followers to accomplish a task, then make it easy for them by asking what resources they need and either providing those resources or giving them directions to find them. Give them a reasonable deadline so they don't feel overwhelmed and lock up. Offer to deal with conflict so they can focus on moving towards achieving their goals. If they don't take action, then make it difficult. Explain that since they haven't purchased your product, they won't be taking the steps towards their goals and you might not be available at a later date to help them. If you have offered a coupon then be sure there is an expiration date.

An important point to consider is that the original project is attainable within the allotted time. The approach of making negative things difficult refers to people who simply are not doing their job. It's a different story if they are working on their project and the delays are unforeseen circumstances that they are processing through. Make things difficult for the people who are not respectful and considerate of your policies. Either they will step up and get in gear, or they'll leave.

A friend of mine who managed her department recently had a situation with a man who was hired as the bookkeeper. He turned out to be lazy and disrespectful. She wanted to fire him, but upper management told her no. She felt in her gut that he was not honest and was manipulating the numbers. This is some serious business, but nonetheless, her superiors did not want to hear what she was saying. Instead of using direct force with him, which produced aggressive behaviors towards her, she started making things difficult for him. Rather than doing the small things to pick up his slack, she let his work sit so that he continued to get further behind. She ignored his aggressive behaviors by leaving every time his voice escalated or he displayed aggressive actions such as slamming papers on the desk. In this way, she was setting her boundaries and letting him know she would not tolerate that behavior. He was trying to use force to get her approvals, but she would not succumb to that behavior. Her superiors eventually questioned her as to why his work was slacking, and she gently reminded them that he was disrespectful and insubordinate. She continued to not enable his laziness, and carefully documented everything.

One Monday morning, when she opened the office, she knew immediately that something was wrong. He had removed all financial documents for the whole year, six months' worth. He stole over $25,000. He wiped clean his computer and had stolen boxes of equipment and product. The police were called. She stood out as the person who dealt with a situation that hurt the whole company. She foresaw a bad situation, made life difficult for him when he did not behave appropriately, and eventually he left. Her work environment is now free of angry outbursts, deceptive practices, and negative co-workers. She was commended for her wise insight.

You might be wondering exactly what actions to take to make the wrong road difficult and the right road easy. I won't outline specific steps because each situation is different. I *can* tell you that if one of your team members or clients is creating conflict, then you can follow these basic steps:

1. Have a casual conversation with the person. Ask a few open-ended vague questions to see if they will offer any information. For instance, ask how he or she feels about your product or service, not about you personally. Then, be quiet and listen. What you're looking for is something that's happening outside of work that is a distraction. Maybe

their health is a challenge. Maybe they're in a rough relationship and contemplating divorce. Maybe they are also caring for an elderly parent. These life events can seriously affect a person's attitude and behaviors and should be dealt with, but not in the same way as someone who consistently shows up with Gunslinger Syndrome.

2. If you learn nothing from the casual conversation, call a formal meeting between you and the other person. Send them an email so you have the paper trail. Set a brief agenda, including why you want to meet. For example, tell them you feel like there's some conflict and would like to discuss it with them in order to get it resolved so that the team can increase productivity. Short and simple is the way to be. When you meet, simply ask how they feel about your product or service. Then sit and listen. Take some notes. They might have some really good insight that you don't have. Or, if they are an aggressive person, see step 4.

3. Always end every meeting with an agreement of some sort. So many times meetings end because time is up. Being respectful of time is most certainly important. If you're nearing your end time, simply move to the agreement and action plan phase or agree to have another meeting. Agree to make your product or service right if there was a

problem on your end. Give them a date by which you will have the situation repaired. If you were truly not responsible for the problem, then let them know that's how you see the situation and why, but continue to seek a resolution with them. You will set your boundaries and they will know you care about them.

4. If the other person is simply an aggressive person who wants to engage in aggressive behavior, either active or passive, then you should end the meeting until they can agree to seek a solution in a calm, respectful manner. Respect your own boundaries and code so that they can choose to do so also. Your goal is to stand out as a problem solver.

Remember, a solution must be a win for every party involved. That means that every person must understand that his or her solution is not *the* winning solution but part of a greater solution. Sometimes it's tempting to go with one person's solution simply because it takes time and energy to create a better solution. It's the one that seems the best. If all parties are not happy then it's not the best and will still continue to cause conflict. The relationships will be scarred and continue to hold tension.

Choose your words carefully and choose your body language and facial expressions even more carefully. Have you ever walked away from a meeting where you felt slighted but couldn't figure out why because the other person was so kind? Well they were probably using a softer, lower tone of voice, speaking at a slower rate, smiling, and had open body language all while telling you how your idea, product, or service would never work, and nobody would even consider it because it completely lacked feasibility. Their words were not necessarily nice, and they weren't looking to help, but their tone and body language was warm and endearing. It was a mixed message and certainly not effective for creating solutions, so do not be like that. It leaves a bad aftertaste in people's mouths. Instead, be kind and respectful, slow to speak, and do not interrupt anyone. If you don't feel that you had ample time to talk, simply say that you need to express your concerns and wait your turn.

If you feel that the other person did not care or hear anything you said, then schedule another meeting after you both have had some time to process the conflict. Ask them to come prepared with some different solutions that haven't yet been discussed. Time will give you both the opportunity to create other solutions considering each other's perspectives. This is where the win-win-win solution can be found. This is about navigating the trail with finesse.

A cowgirl doesn't race down a rocky trail through the woods heading off the side of the mountain. That would be sheer stupidity, unless of course a mad grizzly is chasing her. Even then, she'll do her best to navigate the ground along with her horse. They are a team. Most likely, she'll take her time, always checking her surroundings, giving her horse his head so he can see where he needs to place his hooves for each step. Sometimes they'll jog along the trail when the path is sandy and smooth. Sometimes each step is navigated over large rocks and across fallen branches. This is how you should view your journey to business growth. You're navigating a trail, watching for small obstacles to either go around, or larger obstacles that need to be examined and solved. As you navigate your trail, which will involve learning conflict resolution skills, you will stand out as the leader and problem solver.

Solution creation is an important learned skill. It needs to be a winning solution for every party, not simply picking the best one brought to the table. It should be obvious that no one solution is feasible because there is a conflict between parties. One person or several people don't think the best solution is the best. The team gets stalled because people can't agree on one of the solutions. I say quit wasting time arguing over those solutions. Clearly, none of them work for everyone. Not only that, when you sit and argue, your brain is in its analytical left side. It's looking at things as black or white, good or bad, yes or no. People get stuck in the standstill, ready to draw their guns. They are standing on the dirt road, Main Street, of the old west town waiting for someone to draw first. When that happens, all heck breaks loose, and everyone ends up yelling and throwing papers. What would happen if you didn't draw your gun, but instead sat and watched? You would learn a lot.

Sitting and watching and being curious are where you want to be. You will hear why each person feels a solution will or will not work. Not only that if you choose curiosity, you'll be switching on the creative right side of your brain. You have a much better chance of creating a winning solution than the people arguing, attacking others' solutions, and defending their own. The point is to take all the good points that people are defending, erase the non-viable points, and create a winning solution from everyone's input.

It is possible, while difficult, to do this in the midst of a heated meeting or conversation. You will need to practice acting intentionally. As you listen to the conversations, write down the winning ideas from each solution and present those as your solution. Give credit to other team members. Ask them how else the solution can be made better. Try to get them to shift into their creative right brain by asking open-ended questions so that they can think up new and better ideas. You do not have to be the Boss Mare to help turn a meeting in a positive direction. This will help you stand out in a positive light. You're not being controlling. You're simply trying to solve the problem. Always end with asking what they think about the direction you have just suggested. You don't want to look like you're stepping all over anybody's feet. You want to look like a leader and problem-solver, while acting respectfully towards your people.

When trying to solve problems, another tip that will help immensely is to consider what syndrome each person is choosing. When you know what syndrome they have chosen, you can approach them appropriately. If someone is a Gunslinger, then you know you can't be direct because they'll draw their guns and shoot before you even finish your sentence. If someone is the Packhorse, you don't want to be fast and impersonal because they will shut down feeling that the load is unbearable. It's important to study the syndromes so you know the attitudes of your followers and supporters. Once you identify their attitudes, it's so much easier to approach them.

Acknowledgment and Validation

One skill that works like magic to approach anyone in a negative syndrome and to diffuse their attitude is that of acknowledgment and validation. Tell them the positive things they are doing. Tell them how they matter and point out their traits or actions that have made a difference. Then give them some validation around what their feeling or how they're acting. This helps to diffuse that attitudinal energy so they can let it go. They will be drawn to you like a moth to the flame. This is not the same thing as buttering someone up. That feels fake and we all can see it as fraudulent behavior. Acknowledging and validating is something that is sorely lacking in the business arena, heck, in life in general.

So how do you acknowledge and validate? It's two simple sentences.

The first is to point out in a genuine way their positive contribution. This is not flattery or buttering up. It is simply stating what they are doing that is beneficial. Here's an example: *You are really putting a lot of effort into your part of the team's project.*

The second sentence is the validation. It's taking whatever feeling they appear to have and making it normalized. This is why it is especially important to know their syndrome so you can identify the feeling they are having. Here's an example of something to say to someone who is engaged in Packhorse syndrome: *It makes total sense that you're upset that they don't see all the work you've been doing.*

Now you can leave the person with the acknowledgment and validation and walk away from the conversation. That might help because it will at least help the person gain some awareness around their attitude. Believe me, this in itself is helpful for diffusing conflict because people can start to move from their negative attitude to a better, more productive attitude.

You can follow up your two sentences with a simple open-ended question to prompt them to start creating solutions. You could ask what advice they would tell their best friend who came to them with the same problem. You can also ask what their gut is telling them to do. There are many open-ended questions to ask.

There are two keys to asking good open-ended questions. One is to ask one question at a time and then be quiet. If it's a really good question, then the other person needs some time for their brain to switch from the left to the right, process the information, and begin to create a new solution. You might feel as if you can hear a pin drop and that the clock has slowly ticked forward three hours. I guarantee that this gift of silence will propel the person forward out of negativity and conflict faster than anything else you can do. If minutes pass and there is still no response, I usually offer to be available when the person wants to continue the conversation. Many times, after I walk away, the person will show up within five minutes with a revelation. If not, then I check in the following day. The second key is to avoid using the word "I." I realize that goes against many conflict resolution manuals and against the world of psychology. There's a small difference that ends up being big. I'll explain.

In conflict resolution, most people are in Gunslinger mode, attacking the other party for something. Mainstream resolvers feel that by telling people to use "I" statements, then the attacks on the other party will stop. So, experts claim that saying "I feel as if you're not hearing me" won't be an attack. It's still an attack, just not a direct bullet to the face. It's more like a bullet to the arm. It also takes the spotlight off of the Gunslinger. But, that's the spotlight they are seeking, so give it to them, but in a loving and serving way rather than as a gunfight.

What I am suggesting is to first get out of your own head and your left brained defense-attack mode. Be curious about the other person because ultimately this gives you your inner cowgirl power. You are rising above the conflict and choosing to actively create a solution. To diffuse another person's overwhelming feeling or anger, you want to keep the acknowledgment and validation focused on them. The minute you take over and point the light on you, then you've lost control. You've shifted everything to you, and that won't help them to let go of their negativity. By saying, "I think," or "I know," or "I've thought for a long time," you are letting them know how smart you are, not at all helping them to release their negativity. In fact, they'll walk away feeling even worse, either more hopeless or angrier for once again not feeling heard.

Conflict resolution is a huge field with conflicting information. It's funny to me that negotiators can't even agree on the best methods. The best thing for you to do is to master the acknowledgment and validation skills and have a pocketful of open-ended questions you can go to when you are engaged in a conflict.

Here are some questions you can use to help diffuse negative energy:

- It sounds like you're really angry over this situation. What would make it better?
- You seem pretty angry. How can this situation work better for you?
- You seem pretty overwhelmed. What do you need to feel better?
- What can be done to fix this?
- What end result would you like to see?

Being curious is the best way to be because that's when you learn the most. Knowledge gives you power. Using these conflict resolution skills will make you stand out as a leader faster than any other skill because conflict resolution is needed every day and most people are not comfortable with resolution. Most people would prefer to stay stuck in their conflict. Choose to be the leader who specializes in solutions.

12

COFFEE, CANDY BARS, AND TEAM CAMARADERIE

The only way to drive cattle fast is slowly.

Your journey into your new business may be fast or slow. As you navigate that path, you need to keep yourself motivated and your followers engaged because let's face it, building a business takes energy and grit. You feel knocked down at times and have to pick yourself up because at the end of the day, you simply can't quit and go back to the mundane daily grind without your horses.

A key piece to know is that ultimately you can't force your followers to follow. So, don't get mad or sad when they don't. You create the space and conditions for them to choose to follow. Maybe you've heard the phrase "you can lead a horse to water, but you can't make him drink." It's true. You can't force a horse to drink who doesn't want to drink. He will stand there looking at you or looking at the horizon. He might submerge his muzzle into the water only to splash around and get you wet. You simply can't force him to drink. It's the same with your people. You can provide the space, time, and resources, but you can't force them to be stimulated and inspired to jump in.

Just like I spoke about in the last chapter, you make it easy for your people to want to engage and difficult for them to be lazy. I'm going to expand on the concept of making it easy for them to engage and give them reasons to want to be with you. There are many ways to accomplish this, and different experts will have different ways that are important to them. The things I am sharing are basic ways to keep your people supporting you. Remember, this might be for your followers, or it might be for your personal support team who is helping you create awareness and get promoted. These actions help with any team development.

Share your beliefs, vision, and goals. By letting your team know what is motivating you and where you are trying to go, they will be more likely to engage and help. People are more likely to support you if you share your inner passion and beliefs. It's not as engaging to support someone who simply wants more money, but when your true followers have the same beliefs and values as yours, then they will be loyal and supportive. Every ship needs a captain. Every herd needs an alpha leader. A team functions better if they know in what direction they are headed. It provides a sense of security and allows them to get excited about the journey. They can see their part and feel a better sense of belonging if they know the underlying mission and vision for the team's journey.

Communicate with your team on a regular basis. If these are your followers, then you need to be communicating daily in some form or another. Daily social media posts are a great tool for touching base about new things that arise, planning the day, and general communication. For your personal team that is supporting your business building journey, check in weekly, or more. You don't want to be pesky with your personal team, but you do want to foster and nurture those relationships. Checking in could be a quick text to see how they are. It could be an email, a quick phone call, or a cup of coffee. Sometimes surprising them with a cup of coffee or a sweet treat from a bakery is a nice way to let them know you are thinking about them.

Communication should be transparent and authentic. People can tell if you really care by how well you listen. When they talk about their kids, remember their kids' names. Even if you have to keep a journal, write down little facts about your people so they know you hear them and are paying attention. You don't want them to feel invisible, or they will become so. I can't always remember all these facts at the end of the day, so I carry a small pocket notebook that has pages with each person's name and personal facts about them, from their spouses names, children's names, pets' names, favorite stores and restaurants, and any other tidbit of information. If I need a conversation starter, then I can simply ask how their spouse or kids are doing and call them by name. Know how they take their coffee or if they prefer tea. These may seem trivial, but they will know without a doubt that you care and that speaks volumes. If I've worked with or for someone for a year, or even six months, and they can't spell my name correctly, I know I mean very little to them.

Give positive feedback and rewards for exhibiting the behavior you seek in your people. If your team exerts a large, focused effort, then let them know you see it. If I'm loading a young horse into a trailer for the first time, I'll praise him and give him a pat on the neck after he moves forward and steps into the trailer. When he's fully loaded with the partition closed, then he gets the reward of eating hay from a hay bag.

The rewards for your team members don't need to be big. People thrive on receiving credit and accolades. My gosh, most people are starved of genuine compliments and acknowledgment of any kind. Our world is filled with people who have little or no positive support systems, who end up taking anti-depressants because they feel so alone. Don't let your team feel like that. Give credit freely where it's due. Acknowledge effort and give credit for ideas whether they come to fruition or not. You want to keep the positive creative energy freely flowing. Eventually this energy will flow right back to you!

Some of the rewards that I have given in the past were small items. The key is to make sure that the small items are things that have meaning to the recipient. For instance, if I know I'm going to give a small reward to someone, and it's going to be a candy bar, then I make absolute certain that it's the kind they like. Remember the small pocket notebook where I keep personal notations? That would be in there. You might be thinking that a candy bar is hardly a reward. I would probably agree. It probably costs a dollar or two depending on size and brand. It's not really the candy bar that matters. What matters is that I took the time to go buy it, and I paid attention to the fact that it's his or her favorite. That's what matters. I have given candy bars or other candy items many times. I've given coffee in a fancy mug. I've given fruit bowls. I've given a bag of horse treats.

Anything goes. I've also given more expensive gifts if a large goal was reached. Sporting event tickets or concert tickets would be a larger reward. I've held impromptu and unofficial contests where the winner received movie tickets, or a restaurant gift card. I believing in giving rewards often which is why they don't have to be big and fancy. It's the small things on a regular basis that say, "I see you, and I appreciate you" that matter.

Serving others is key to growing your business and getting others to promote you. Even if you teach someone how to do your service, they will still most likely want to hire you to do it because it's serving them and either solving their problem or making their life easier in some way. I've been banding horses' manes since the early 1980s, yet I still pay other people to band my horses at the shows because I just don't want to do it. I can do as good or better than most, but I'd rather pay someone most of the time. So, don't be afraid to share your secrets. People will still pay you for your service.

Welcome feedback. Ask your customers what they think about your product or service. Some people might think this opens them up to appearing weak. It does the opposite. It takes a strong leader to ask his or her followers for feedback. It also takes a wise leader because then you'll know what they want from you, what's working, and what's not. Feedback can be in the form of a meeting, but it's better to get feedback either one-on-one or in writing. Send an online survey link, give them a stamped postcard, or even set up an anonymous suggestion box at an event. Sure, some people will write silly things, but you will also get some good ideas.

Create a safe environment where communication, failure, and misfire are not punished, but instead where they're viewed as opportunities for growth and learning. You don't want your people afraid to share because fear squelches creativity and growth. If something fails, do not cast blame on yourself or others. I want people motivated to help me and to go the extra mile to promote me. If I'm riding a horse and I start whipping and beating on him to give more, he might give some more, but he'll also get mad and eventually either try to buck me off, or just simply quit on me. If I coax him, while asking and releasing the pressure when he gives, then he's more likely to want to serve me and give every time I ask. Releasing the pressure when he steps in the direction I want is how I keep him moving forward in a positive direction. People are the same.

Rotate repetitive and mundane tasks as needed. These tasks are usually entry-level tasks or very technical tasks that will eat up your time. These might be things like website maintenance, email marketing, bookkeeping, or any other task in your daily to-do list that you don't find fun. Outsourcing these tasks is usually worth the money because they will take you three times as long to complete them and suck the energy from your spirit. You don't want to give up either of those things. Instead, focus on the parts of your business that excite you and make your soul sing and your spirit dance. That's what will keep you motivated and keep your followers attracted to you like moths to a light.

Share your personal goals and ask your people to share theirs. If they don't have goals, help them make their goals and create an action plan. Whether these are your followers or your personal team, the fact that you take an interest in someone else's goals shows them that you care. This helps build loyalty. Some people have big scary goals, and some have smaller goals. Support them and they will be much more likely to support you.

Celebrate the wins. While this is similar to giving rewards, the wins being celebrated are bigger. They are situations or challenges that have been overcome. They are not simply meeting a deadline or accomplishing a task. The real wins include overcoming something and reaching the goal. It doesn't just mean when someone wins a class or rides their bronc. Look at the wins in life such as overcoming a life challenge or someone else launching a business. This might look like applauding them on your social media, emailing your list of followers, or showing up in person with balloons or cookies. Applaud them in front of others. Make it look like a celebration.

Promote team camaraderie. You want your team members to like each other. They don't need to be buddies outside of your team, but they do need to feel a sense of unity. Team building is a huge area with much written on the subject, so explore this in depth. You want to become the person who also helps others make connections. For instance, if you are banding and braiding at shows and see that someone is struggling with a horse that has some soundness issues, you can suggest a really good farrier, or a PEMF practitioner, or a good vet. Have your list of people so you can share them and help solve a problem. The more you refer, the more referrals you'll get.

Always remember to have fun! Always being serious saps the fun out of the day and the life out of your team. People like to laugh. When was the last time you laughed? I mean really laughed, not just some chuckle. Maybe you can't even remember. Laughter is important, and most people don't get enough of it. So, infuse laughter into your marketing, your communications, and your mistakes. We all know that laughter is the best medicine, but we don't always take that medicine. So be intentional and try to make others laugh. They'll want to be around you more and will become your loyal followers quicker.

Perhaps the most important key to remember is that when your people are excited and engaged, their energy will feed you and then your positive energy will be tuned into them, creating a back and forth flow of energy. This is what keeps you motivated to continue serving them and what keeps them continually engaged. If that balance sways too far to one side, then either you or your people will get drained and eventually quit. Because you are the one building the business, you must start the exchange. This is done by serving them, finding out what they need most, and filling that need. Don't overcomplicate this.

Building and nurturing relationships between team members also creates a cohesive, motivated team. Sitting around a campfire, sipping coffee or hot chocolate on a cool night while staring into the red-orange dancing flames is a great way to learn about your team and their goals, desires, passions, and challenges. Coffee around the campfire is an amazing thing. While we cannot all do that, we can create similar situations such as virtual events or physical retreats so that we can fully learn who our people are and how to engage them for the long run.

13

GETTING TURFED

*Confidence is the feeling you have
before you understand the situation.*

etting turfed is when you hit the ground hard and fast immediately after getting bucked off. Every cowgirl who has ridden has gotten turfed at some point. Nonetheless, a cowgirl dusts off her britches and swings her leg over her horse again. Anyone who has worked in business has gotten turfed a time or two also. You've been knocked down a rung or two, feeling like a crash and burn hit you from behind. Sometimes you feel overwhelmed and defeated. Sometimes you feel cheated.

Dusting off your Wranglers, holding your chin up high, and strutting back into the arena is what you must do in order to hold onto your sanity and self-respect, as well as your paycheck. Let's take a look at some of the things that trip you as you build your dream business.

Although there are many events, actions, or relationships that may cause you to fail or scramble, your attitude has by far the biggest impact on your own success. That may seem harsh, but you need to understand the importance of being aware of your attitude so that you can make your choices from a place of consciousness rather than from fear, anger, or self-pity. Assessing your own attitude is certainly difficult. Some of us are extra hard on ourselves, and some of us excuse and justify our actions and words quite easily. Holding up a mirror to yourself never seems to be quite accurate.

So, how can you hold up a mirror so you can objectively observe your attitude, without the reflection appearing wonky like the carnival funhouse mirrors that seek to distort perceptions and startle you with unpredictable reflections?

Let's start with identifying your strengths and weaknesses, which might be a bit easier than accurately assessing your attitude. There are several online personality assessments that you can take to shed light on your personality type. When I was director of operation assessment for a medium sized corporation, I ran an off-brand assessment on all managers. We used the assessment for training to increase a person's awareness of him or herself. I used other tools to identify knowledge gaps so that training could be focused on the gaps as well as increasing the strengths.

There are many assessments that you can find on the Internet. The most important part of doing the assessment is interpreting the results and formulating next steps. An objective outsider who can help you look at yourself in an accurate manner does this process best. I truly believe that paying a professional coach or consultant will give you far better results than asking friends and family who are either your cheerleaders or your baggage handlers.

Let's look again at some of the syndromes and how you might show up to your customers and supporters. You need to show up and stand out in a positive, punchy manner so that you're the obvious choice. You can see some of the obstacles by looking at the syndromes. The Round Pen Syndrome has a person doing a lot of tasks. There is a lot of movement and action, which can appear high energy and high-achieving. However, the challenge is that the energy is really just being used to run in circles. You're not moving forward. You're doing a lot of work, and you probably look like you're moving up, but in reality, you might not have healthy boundaries and find yourself being taken advantage of and used. Stopping this syndrome is difficult for several reasons.

When you're in the round pen and taking on a lot of free work, people rely on you and that feels good. You feel needed and important. You put up with some things, though, that keep you in the round pen rather than blazing your own trail. And, it's tough to get that gate open and gain respect because feeling needed provides security. Fear keeps you in the round pen. There's fear that if you say no or charge people money for your service, then they'll walk away or laugh at you. If you're kept in the round pen, then everyone else is comfortable too, knowing where you are and passing his or her work onto you. You are spending a lot of time giving stuff away, and making very little money. When we give away our products or services, we are telling people that they aren't all that valuable. We are coming from an attitude of scarcity and fear. This attitude is difficult to change on your own.

The next syndrome is the Cowgirl Strong Syndrome. Even though the Cowgirl Strong Syndrome is a positive syndrome, there can be obstacles within this syndrome. This is a great syndrome because this is where problem solvers reside. You can look at a situation, assess it without getting angry or casting blame, and work on formulating solutions. You are a great team leader because you don't play games. The challenge with this syndrome occurs when there are so many juicy solutions that you simply can't choose one. The person who generally shows up with this syndrome is a high-achiever, quick thinker, and action-taker most of the time. Occasionally, you will spend too much time analyzing a situation and then get stuck in the analysis phase, failing to move into the action phase. Sometimes you are the perfectionist, and sometimes you simply are unable to choose which solution to put into action. Many times, a good nudge gets you moving. Sometimes you don't even realize you are stuck in the decision phase because you think that analysis is wise. And it is. But there's a fine line between being stuck in the analysis phase and taking action.

Another challenge that can happen with the Cowgirl Strong Syndrome is frustration. You might be standing on the open range, looking at all the possibilities and directions you can go. You see the wide-open horizon and know that you can conquer anything you set your mind to, but you are standing there holding your hat in one hand and scratching your head with your other hand… thinking…dreaming…imagining…creating. The sun goes down before you've taken any steps forward onto a trail. Or, you might have your trail chosen. You know exactly in which direction you need to go to navigate the mountain ahead, but your posse wants to campout right where they are sitting. Your frustration mounts, eventually turning to anger. Dealing with the frustration of not moving forward is tormenting at best, and complete failure at worst.

The last syndrome I will address is the Rodeo Bronc Syndrome. This can be a crash and burn if you're not careful. A cowgirl can be riding the bucking bronc, feeling in total synch as the 1,500 pounds of flesh underneath her jumps, dives, and kicks out. She feels her heart pounding from excitement. She has no fear because she knows she's got this. Suddenly, the hooves hit the ground in an unexpected crash of hoof to dust, the horse twists, and she catapults off the side. As a business woman, this has happened to you too, I'd bet. You're working on a project, feeling like you and your followers are in synch with ideas freely flowing. On Monday morning, you arrive at work only to learn that half of your followers quit. You feel as if the rug was pulled out from under your feet. You can hardly process the situation and feel like there's simply no point in working so hard and giving so much of yourself to others.

What has happened is that you were working, fully engaged with your intuition and in your flow, almost with your head in the clouds. You weren't grounded and paying attention to the small unspoken things happening around you. You heard the feedback that you wanted to hear, but not some of the feedback that didn't fit into your plan.

When a cowgirl rides a bucking horse, it's important to feel all parts of the animal. All four hooves are off the ground at the same time, so in order to stay on, she has to anticipate where and when those hooves hit the ground so she can stay grounded. Flying high with the bucks is fun, but being grounded is key to balancing and staying on. Beating the hooves to the ground is anticipating where and when they land so you don't get catapulted right out of the saddle like a jellybean out of a slingshot.

When you're focusing on a project in your business, this same concept applies. Of course, it's great to be tuned into your intuition and flow as you solve problems and bring ideas to life, but you still must stay grounded and alert to the unspoken movements of your followers. You need to look up once in a short while and refocus your vision to see what's happening with those around you. What are people whispering? What is going on in the industry? People might be having conversations with your followers that could prompt them to cast that death blowing unfollow click with you. Look for the nuances and small changes in people's behavior. Certainly, if people are avoiding you, then look closer at what is happening with them and how you can better serve them through your products or services.

So how can you increase your self-awareness, learn conflict resolution skills, learn to identify and navigate the syndromes, and apply all the skills that we've discussed? You can do the exercises, create an action plan, find a mentor and accountability partner, identify resources, and take your first action plan steps. The challenges that most people face are that they either fizzle out before experiencing results, they choose inappropriate mentors and poor accountability partners, or life gets in the way, so they completely excuse themselves from the journey.

Many years ago, I was not a fan of finding a coach. I felt that people who needed coaches were weak. I also thought that coaches were the next big craze, and everyone was calling him or herself a coach. Certainly, there are a lot of people who do the internet coaching programs and are coaches overnight. Becoming anything overnight is not wise. A master has to fail many, many times before fully understanding the process and then being able to lead others through the process.

You can choose to try to navigate the business arena on your own, but I'd guess that you'll most likely stay in the bucking chute or move at a snail's pace. I recommend finding a coach who has graduated from a well-known coaching program, or a coach who has been highly recommended by someone that you know. Don't rely solely on a great marketing page.

A certified professional coach is not going to tell you what you should do, although they might point in some directions for you to consider. What they will do is help you to better understand where you are on your journey, how you are holding yourself back and tripping yourself up, and then how to stand out like a punchy leader. Some of the side effects of coaching you through your business launch are that you will see your personal relationships change as well. You will not only be setting boundaries for professional relationships, but you will find that you can more easily set boundaries in personal relationships. When you learn to say no in a professional arena, you are saying yes to yourself and your time. This is the same in the personal arena.

Perhaps the most powerful part of coaching is uncovering the roadblocks that are holding you back. So, when you fail to move forward and take action on a task or relationship, a coach will help you uncover what is keeping you from stepping into action. When these blocks are removed, you gain a new, fresh perspective and are better qualified to be the leader that you know resides inside. Your coach will help you stay focused on your goals and navigate the difficulties that will arise both in yourself and along your path. Your inner cowgirl will stand up and help you lead yourself more effectively so that you can successfully serve and lead others.

14

PROMOTE YOUR INNER COWGIRL

You are confined only by the fences you build yourself.

I am super excited for you to embark on your journey so that you can launch a business following your passion that gives you more time with your horses. This is not just a possibility. When you implement the steps in this book, you will be able to launch a business that earns you money and gives you more time to spend with your horses. Let's review those steps.

1. **Your Cowgirl Code**: You created your personal policy manual outlining your goals, boundaries,

and passions to ensure that the promotion you desire is in alignment with who you are.

2. **Your Arena**: You identified who is playing in your arena, who your supporters are, and who is in the crowd watching (your followers).

3. **Your Syndrome**: You identified your main syndrome, describing how you show up to your people. You also examined how those around you show up in response to you.

4. **Meet Your Inner Cowgirl**: You learned how to stand out as a leader and team player by tapping into your inner cowgirl. You learned some positive syndromes as guides for standing out.

5. **Cowgirl Grit**: You looked at past successes and failures, learning how to refocus your vision into a new perspective that uses your past to launch you into your business.

6. **From Cowboss to CEO**: You created your ideal job description, examined your personal brand, and identified needs and resources to get you into the business you seek.

7. **Creating Your Posse**: You identified who is on your team of supporters and how to build that team.

8. **Herding Your Humans**: You identified some conflict resolution skills that you can use to diffuse conflict around you.

9. **Campfire Coffee**: You learned how to keep yourself motivated and your team actively engaged.

10. **Obstacles**: You learned what obstacles could arise and how to overcome them swiftly.

The syndromes that you will see in your business arena are the following:

- **Packhorse Syndrome**: You do most of the work for the team because everyone dumps on you. They know you'll take it without a fight. You feel unappreciated and under-valued. Eventually you wear out and feel hopeless.

- **School Horse Syndrome**: This is similar to Packhorse Syndrome except you get an accolade and pats on the back every now and then, just enough to keep you moderately hopeful, or so you tell yourself. People love you, but at the end of the day, they stick you in a stall and walk away until they need you again because you don't really belong to anyone. You don't have a loyal base of followers.

- **Gunslinger Syndrome**: The Gunslingers are all over corporate America. They show up with guns drawn, ready to push their agenda, and take what they believe is theirs, regardless of whom they step on or over. They love a fight and make people gun shy without much effort. They get results, but only because people are fearful of getting shot in the back. Even bystanders take cover for fear of catching a stray bullet.

- **Round Pen Syndrome**: You do a fair amount of work and get some things accomplished, checking them off your list. However, you don't really move forward because you're simply doing a lot of busy work. You produce average results at best. You're really just dabbling in your business – or is it a hobby? You give away more than you earn. Eventually you fizzle out and become angry with yourself and others, reverting to a Gunslinger and pulling your guns out of your holsters.

- **Boss Mare Syndrome**: You come across as the strong leader. You like being in control. You are well organized, delegate swiftly, and produce results. As quickly as you show compassion, you also can lash out. Sometimes you come across as bossy. When you get frustrated from others' lack of swift production, you tend to get angry and aggressive. Everyone thinks you're a good leader, except when you get upset, kick out, and sulk away.

- **Cowgirl Strong Syndrome**: You are a problem solver. You analyze situations and find solutions with savvy and expertise. You are a fun leader who gets the job done and treats her people with compassion. You communicate

often and well. Sometimes you get tripped up
with over analyzing and don't put your visionary ideas into action.

- **Rodeo Bronc Syndrome**: You are intuitive and
self-aware. You can read most people easily and
delight in settling into your flow, forgetting about
time and deadlines. Sometimes your head is a
bit too far in the clouds with your dreams taking
over reality. You need grounding before you get
burned out.

As you navigate your business-building journey,
remember that your mindset on the journey is paramount
to choosing your attitude and how you will choose to
respond to the challenges in your business. Raising your
level of awareness comes through observing your syndromes and the syndromes of those around you. Once
you identify these syndromes, your journey becomes so
much easier. The energy that these syndromes hold is
dissipated through seeing them as they are. That is half
of the battle that you face each day. As you grow and
develop your keen ability to see underneath a person's
behavior, including your own, you will gain the power
to positively influence the people around you so that you
get what you need and want without trampling on those
around you or being trampled.

Remember the herding chapter? There is a point
rider who leads, flank riders who hold the herd together,

and a drag rider who keeps the stragglers close to the herd. When you are aware of your people and their syndromes, it's as if you're riding all spots at once. You know immediately if a Gunslinger has entered the meeting and instead of engaging the Gunslinger in a ruthless battle, you might ask what's on his mind in order to disengage his trigger finger. If a Boss Mare walks in, then you know you can acknowledge and validate her ideas and opinions before proceeding so that she feels valued, heard, and in control.

You maintain the power because you are aware of the emotional state of yourself and your people. This skill takes time to hone but will swiftly sling your business up the ladder of success once you are adept at using it. Along the way, be sure to acknowledge your wins, no matter how small. Validate yourself as if you were talking to your best friend. No matter what, keep flinching forward through each buck, and pretty soon, you'll be beating the hooves to the ground and riding through the bucks with a big yahoo!

Act with a grateful attitude as if you have already built your dream business. Appreciate the good qualities in those around and you will see those characteristics grow. If you nurture the good in others you help them to shine, and many times they shine their light right back on you. This is how followers promote you. They shed light on all the good things you do and say.

Choose authenticity. You must know who you are before you can be authentic with others. Figure out what your default syndrome is when you are stressed or feeling defeated. Then choose a better syndrome. Visualize what it would be like to be the leader, the problem solver, and the one to whom others gravitate toward for advice and guidance. Then simply start acting like that leader.

You may have failed in your past business ventures because you probably showed up as the Packhorse or Gunslinger. You either appeared weak and flimsy, or like a loose cannon. The Packhorse gets no respect and the Gunslinger appears crazy and unstable. The business world is one of respect. Therefore, set your boundaries, say no in a matter of fact manner, and treat others kindly and firmly.

One day soon you will let your inner cowgirl rise up and show yourself, and others, how to lead with compassion, grit, and savvy. This is the woman who stands out as the punchy cowgirl, full of spirit, able to see the opportunities all around, and led by her intuition and wisdom. Whether you ride horses, have ridden, or simply dream of riding one day, when you let your inner cowgirl stand out and lead the way, then you've earned your spurs. So, cowgirl, strap on your spurs, Cowgirl Up, and let's ride!

ACKNOWLEDGMENTS

This book has been a very long time in the making, brewing in my soul and waiting for the right time to stand out. I needed to traverse through some life challenges so that I could remember who I am and honor my intuition. Some of life's lessons take longer than others. I spent five years wrestling with myself so that I could see through the garbage into the truth, in spite of things I was told. So many people played a part in my journey, pushing me, pulling me, and making me tougher and wiser along the way. For those lessons, I am grateful.

To The Author Incubator team: Special thanks again to Angela Lauria, CEO & Founder of The Author Incubator, for believing in me, seeing my real message and fearlessly leading my tender spirit. To my Developmental Editor, Mehrina Asif, and Managing Editors, Todd Hunter and Nkechi Obi, thanks for making the process seamless and easy. Many more thanks to everyone else at TAI, but especially Cheyenne Giesecke and Ramses Rodriguez for your support and guidance.

Thank you to David Hancock and the Morgan James Publishing team for helping me bring this book to print.

To Heather and Dave: You are my people. You have taught me what friendship and loyalty truly mean. You have shown me unconditional love and support and modeled friendship in ways that would have never crossed my mind. I am forever grateful for the lessons you have taught me and honored by how you continually show up in my life. I love you both.

To Michael: This happened because you asked that one question on that phone call. *Where will you be next year if you don't do this now?* Thank you for your insight and for pushing me just enough so that I took that first step.

To my former and current employers: Without you, I would not have had the countless opportunities to learn compassionate communication and to hone leadership skills. Thank you for believing in me, supporting my growth and development, and promoting me into jobs I loved.

To my amazing clients: Thank you for showing up each week and trusting me with your innermost challenges as you traverse your journeys. Thank you for being brave enough to be transparent and honest. I love every minute of our work together and am honored that you have chosen to allow me to accompany you on your transformational journey. Love and hugs!

Thank you to Jeff G., Peppy and Jeff C. for training my horses and my children so that I had the time to pursue my education and write this book, while still having the time to sit in the saddle and fill my soul. Your hard work and long hours are not invisible. Sharing your camper and opening your home to my girls is a huge investment you have made in my future leaders. Thank you, thank you!

To my parents: Thank you for hanging on as I continually pushed the limits in my life. Without you, none of this would be possible. You scooped me up at my lowest, and continually remind me to celebrate my wins. I'm sure I've been the tiring middle child, so I pray for you to be filled with joy and energy. I love you both!!

Finally, to my children, Cori, Emma, and Tom: You are my everything. You have taught me to love deeply and unconditionally. You are the future of this world, and I pray that you each find your people and lead fearlessly and compassionately. I pray that with each challenge, you are able to look at it, and find the hidden lesson so that you needn't revisit the challenge wrapped in a different package. Most of all, I pray that you find your passion and live your life playing big in your arena. I love you each…no favorites!!!!!

THANKS FOR READING

Thank You!

I am honored that you chose to read *Promote Your Inner Cowgirl: The Horse Lover's Way to Work Less, Earn More, and Live Your Passion*. I know that because you have finished reading this book you are ready to launch your dream job. No more long work hours and missed time with your horses!

As a special thank you, I have created a free class that you can take today to assess your attitude and transform your life. Each morning for seven days, you will receive a punchy, focused video by email to start your day. Grab your coffee and sign up at www.CowgirlBusinessSchool.com.

As part of my personal mission to create future winning leaders, a portion of the proceeds from this book and any of my programs goes to support 4-H Clubs. Thanks for investing in our future leaders!

ABOUT THE AUTHOR

D r. Lynda Flowers is a serial entrepreneur, certified professional coach, and certified family
nurse practitioner. Her past and current positions also include licensed realtor, a massage therapist,

a chiropractic assistant, a nail technician, a registered nurse, a certified obstetrics sonographer, energy leadership master practitioner, director of operations, and director of operation assessment.

Dr. Lynda believes in giving back to the community through volunteering and service. She was a Boy Scout leader for many years serving as the advancement coordinator and committee member. She led women's Bible study groups for many years at her local church and travelled to Nicaragua four times on medical mission trips. She also volunteers at her local pregnancy center performing ultrasounds and counseling women in crisis pregnancies.

Dr. Lynda has been a single mom for most of her 25 years of parenting. She is raising and launching two daughters and a son to be future leaders. Her daughters show Quarter horses and have amassed more awards than can be listed. One daughter works in corporate America and one has her own successful business. Her son plays football and video games and was recently launched off to college.

Dr. Lynda grew up being a horse-crazy girl and bought her own horse at the tender age of 12. He tried killing her on many occasions, but eventually became her best friend, teacher, and protector. She is a past National Reserve Champion at the collegiate level. She has shown English and Western Pleasure, run barrels, rode with the

University of Aberdeen eventing team in Scotland, roped steers, and chased wild cows and bulls in Utah. In her free time, she reads medical research articles and designs and sews quilts.

Website:
http://CowgirlBusinessSchool.com

Email:
Lynda@CowgirlBusinessSchool.com

Facebook:
https://www.facebook.com/CowgirlBusinessSchool

CPSIA information can be obtained
at www.ICGtesting.com
Printed in the USA
JSHW031107120720
6612JS00001BA/19